Englisch lernen mit **Berlitz**®

IAN RANKIN

Three new Cases for Inspector Rebus

Berlitz Publishing
München • New York • Singapur

Berlitz Englisch lernen mit Ian Rankin
Three new Cases for Inspector Rebus

Vokabelerklärungen und Übungen: Astrid Stannat
Layout: Ute Weber
Cover-Gestaltung: Dominik Lommer
Projektleitung: Eva Betz

Englische Originalausgabe:
Beggars Banquet by Ian Rankin

First published by The Orion Publishing Group, London.

This edition is published by arrangement with Orion.

Berlitz Publishing
Mies-van-der-Rohe-Straße 1
D-80807 München

Satz: Franzis print & media Gmbh, München
Druck: CS-Druck Cornelsen Stürtz, Berlin
Bindung: Stein + Lehmann, Berlin
Printed in Germany
ISBN 978-3-468-79233-5

1. 2. 3. 4. 5.   12 11 10 09 08

Inhalt

Lieber Krimi-Fan,

mit den spannenden Kurzkrimis von Ian Rankin halten Sie endlich ein Englischbuch in der Hand, das Sie garantiert nicht mehr weglegen wollen. Und vor lauter Nervenkitzel merken Sie vielleicht gar nicht, dass Sie ganz nebenbei auch Ihre Englischkenntnisse gehörig auffrischen und erweitern.
Damit Ihr Lesevergnügen nicht durch das Nachschlagen unbekannter Wörter gemindert wird, sind die schwierigsten Vokabeln im Text blau markiert und in der Marginalspalte übersetzt. Interessante Wörter, die in einer Infobox erklärt werden, sind zusätzlich mit einem Sternchen gekennzeichnet. Alle übersetzten Wörter sind außerdem im Wörterverzeichnis im Anhang zusammengefasst.
Allein beim Schmökern in den Krimis können Sie sehr viel dazulernen. Vielleicht möchten Sie aber auch Ihr Grammatikwissen und Ihre Vokabelkenntnisse zusätzlich erweitern oder aber Ihr Textverständnis prüfen. Zu diesem Zweck finden Sie auf jeder Seite knifflige und unterhaltsame Übungen. Die Vokabeln aus dem Text werden dort noch einmal verwendet und bleiben dadurch viel besser im Gedächtnis haften – so können Sie später leichter darauf zurückgreifen. Selbstverständlich sind auch die Lösungen zu allen Übungen im Anhang abgedruckt.
Und nun wünschen wir Ihnen viel Spaß und Spannung beim Lesen!

Ihre Berlitz-Redaktion

Talk Show

AN INSPECTOR REBUS STORY

Lowland Radio was a young but successful station broadcasting to lowland Scotland*. It was said that the station owed its success to two very different personalities. One was the DJ on the mid-morning slot, an abrasive and aggressive Shetland Islander*, called Hamish MacDiarmid. MacDiarmid hosted a phone-in, supposedly concerning the day's headlines, but in fact these were of relatively minor importance. People did not listen to the phone-in for opinion and comment: they listened for the attacks MacDiarmid made on just about every caller. There were occasional fierce interchanges, interchanges the DJ nearly always won by dint of severing the connection with anyone more intelligent, better informed, or more rational than himself.

Radiosender, der … ausstrahlte • verdankte • Sendeplatz • ruppig • moderierte • angeblich

heftig • Wortwechsel • dadurch, dass er … abbrach

info

Das Gebiet zwischen den Städten Edinburgh, Glasgow, Stirling, Perth und Dundee bezeichnet man als Lowlands. Es gilt als das wirtschaftliche und kulturelle Zentrum Schottlands. Die Lowlands liegen zwischen den Southern Uplands, dem südlichen Bergland, das bis zur englisch-schottischen Grenze reicht, und den Highlands, dem gebirgigen Hochland im Norden. Noch weiter im Nordosten, in einiger Entfernung zum Festland, befinden sich die Inselgruppen der Orkney- und Shetland-Inseln.

Rebus knew that there were men in his own station who would try to take a break between ten-forty-five and eleven-fifteen just to listen. The people who phoned the show knew what they'd get, of course: that was part of the fun. Rebus wondered if they were masochists, but in fact he knew they probably saw themselves as challengers. If they could best Mac Diarmid, they would have 'won'. And so MacDiarmid himself became like some raging bull, entering the ring every morning for another joust with the picadors. So far he'd been goaded but not wounded, but who knew how long the luck would last …?

The other 'personality' – always supposing personality could be applied to someone so ethereal – was Penny Cook, the softly spoken, seductive voice on the station's late-night slot. Five nights a week, on her show *What's Cookin'*, she offered a mix of sedative music, soothing talk, and calming advice to those who took part in her own phone-in segment. These were very different people from those who chose to confront Hamish MacDiarmid. They were quietly worried about their lives, insecure, timid; they had home problems, work problems, personal problems. They were the kind

(Polizei-)Revier
Herausforderer • übertreffen • wütend • Stier • Zweikampf • gereizt • anhalten
ätherisch • verführerisch
beruhigend • besänftigend • Ratschläge
unsicher • schüchtern

Übung 1 Sind die folgenden Aussagen wahr oder falsch?
Tragen Sie ein T für true oder ein F für false in die Kästchen ein.

1. ☐ Hamish MacDiarmid hosted a mid-morning radio show.
2. ☐ Lots of people listened to his show because it was rather informative.
3. ☐ Penny Cook's callers were aggressive and troublesome.
4. ☐ Penny offered them advice when they told her about their problems.
5. ☐ Inspector Rebus listened to Penny's show every night.
6. ☐ He did not know what Penny looked like.

of people, Rebus mused, who got sand kicked in their faces. MacDiarmid's callers, on the other hand, were probably the ones doing the kicking …

Perhaps it said something about the lowlands of Scotland that Penny Cook's show was said to be the more popular of the two. Again, people at the station talked about it with the fervour usually reserved for TV programmes.

'Did you hear yon guy with the bend in his tackle …?'

'That woman who said her husband didn't satisfy her …'

'I felt sorry for that hooker though, wantin' out o' the game …'

And so on. Rebus had listened to the show himself a few times, slumped on his chair after closing-time. But never for more than a few minutes; like a bedtime story, a few minutes of Penny Cook sent John Rebus straight to the land of Nod. He'd wondered what she looked like. Husky, comfortable, come-to-bed: the picture of her he'd built up was all images, but none of them exactly physical. Sometimes she sounded blonde and tiny, sometimes statuesque with flowing raven hair. His picture of Hamish MacDiarmid was much more vivid: bright red beard, caber-tossing* biceps and a kilt*.

sinnierte
galt als
Eifer
jenen Kerl • Sprung in der Schüssel • Nutte
zusammengesackt • Sperrstunde • Reich der Träume • rau
wie von klassischer Schönheit • rabenschwarz • leuchtend

info

Bei den traditionellen Highland Games ist der caber toss eine der schwerathletischen Disziplinen. Das Werfen eines circa 5 Meter langen und bis zu 70 Kilogramm schweren Baumstamms erfordert enorme Kraft und Geschicklichkeit. Dabei ist nicht die Weite ausschlaggebend für den Sieg, sondern die Position des geworfenen Stamms. Das schmale Ende des Stamms, das der Wettkampfteilnehmer in den Händen hält, muss nach dem Wurf möglichst senkrecht nach oben zeigen.

Es ist üblich, dass die Teilnehmer der Highland Games im kilt, dem knielangen, karierten Schottenrock, auftreten.

Well, the truth would out. Rebus stood in the cramped reception area of Lowland Radio and waited for the girl on the switchboard to finish her call. On the wall behind her, a sign said WELCOME:. That colon was important. This seemed to be Lowland Radio's way of greeting the personalities who'd come to the station, perhaps to give interviews. Today, below the WELCOME:, written in felt tip were the names JEZ JENKS and CANDY BARR. Neither name meant anything to Rebus, though they probably would to his daughter. The receptionist had finished her call.

'Have you come for some stickers?'

'Stickers?'

'Car-stickers,' she explained. 'Only we're all out of them. Just temporary, we'll be getting more next week if you'd like to call back.'

'No, thanks anyway. I'm Inspector Rebus. I think Miss Cook's expecting me.'

'Oh, sorry.' The receptionist giggled. 'I'll see if she's around. It was Inspector …?'

'Rebus.'

She scribbled the name on a pad and returned to her switchboard. 'An Inspector Reeves to see you, Penny …'

eng • Telefonzentrale • Doppelpunkt • begrüßen • Filzstift • keiner der beiden Namen • wir haben überhaupt keine mehr • vorübergehend • erwartet mich • kicherte • kritzelte • Block

Übung 2 Ergänzen Sie die fehlenden Buchstaben der englischen Begriffe.

1. A _ h _ _ _ f _ _ person is someone who smiles and laughs a lot.
2. You use a _ a _ to write notes.
3. Hamish MacDiarmid's _ n _ _ l _ s (his rude and offensive remarks) did not keep people from calling.
4. Young girls often _ _ g _ _ e when they think that something is funny or when they are nervous.
5. Penny Cook's hair was straight, but as she wanted it to be curly, she got it _ e _ _ e _.

Rebus turned to another wall and cast an eye over Lowland Radio's small display of awards. Well, there was stiff competition these days, he supposed. And not much advertising revenue to go round.

warf einen Blick • Sammlung von Auszeichnungen • Einnahmen

Another local station had countered the challenge posed by Hamish MacDiarmid, hiring what they called 'The Ranter', an anonymous individual who dished out insult upon insult to anyone foolish enough to call his show.

gekontert

austeilte • Beleidigung über Beleidigung

It all seemed a long way from the Light Programme*, a long way from glowing valves and Home Counties* diction. Was it true that the BBC announcers used to wear dinner jackets? DJs in DJs, Rebus thought to himself and laughed.

glühende Röhren

'I'm glad somebody's cheerful.' It was Penny Cook's voice; she was standing right behind him. Slowly he turned to be confronted by a buxom lady in her early forties – only a year or two younger than Rebus himself. She had permed light brown hair and wore round glasses – the kind popularised by John Lennon on one hand and the NHS* on the other.

fröhlich

drall

dauergewellt

'I know, I know,' she said. 'I'm never what people

info

Light Programme nannte sich der Radiosender der BBC, der von 1945 bis 1967 Unterhaltungsmusik ausstrahlte.
Viele Menschen leben in den an London angrenzenden Grafschaften, den Home Counties, und pendeln von dort aus mit dem Zug oder dem Auto zur Arbeit. Die Bewohner der Home Counties gelten als eher konservativ und sind an ihrer Ausdrucksweise (diction) zu erkennen.
Der National Health Service (NHS), die staatliche Gesundheitsorganisation des Vereinigten Königreichs, bietet jedem Einwohner freie ärztliche Versorgung. Ähnlich wie bei uns sind die Kassenbrillengestelle eher schlicht.

	expect.' She held out a hand, which Rebus shook. Not
nicht bedrohlich	only did Penny Cook sound unthreatening, she *looked* unthreatening.
	All the more mysterious then that someone, some
bedrohen	anonymous caller, should be threatening her life …
stabil aussehend	They walked down a corridor towards a sturdy-looking
• angebracht • Tastenfeld •	door, to the side of which had been attached a push-button array.
Ziffern •	'Security,' she said, pressing four digits before pulling
Verrückter •	open the door. 'You never know what a lunatic might
Zugang	do given access to the airwaves.' 'On the contrary,' said Rebus, 'I've heard Hamish MacDiarmid.'
	She laughed. He didn't think he'd heard her laugh before. 'Is Penny Cook your real name?' he asked,
ausreichend •	thinking the ice sufficiently broken between them.
ehrlich gesagt •	'Afraid so. I was born in Nairn. To be honest, I don't
(Stadtteil v. Edinburgh, ausgesprochen wie Penny Cook)	think my parents had heard of Penicuik. They just liked the name Penelope.' They were passing studios and offices. Loudspeakers
• Decke • gaben … wieder	placed in the ceiling of the corridor relayed the station's afternoon show. 'Ever been inside a radio station before, Inspector?'

Übung 3 Welche der angegebenen Möglichkeiten ist die richtige? Kreuzen Sie sie an.

1. In order to get inside the radio station Inspector Rebus had to
- ☐ get a key from the receptionist.
- ☐ pass through a combination-lock door.
- ☐ attach a sticker to his jacket.

2. While he was passing studios and offices, Inspector Rebus could
- ☐ see Hamish MacDiarmid through one of the glass doors.
- ☐ count the loudspeakers in the corridor.
- ☐ hear the station's afternoon programme.

'No, never.'
'I'll show you around if you like.'
'If you can spare the time …'
'No problem.' They were approaching one studio outside which a middle-aged man was in quiet conversation with a spiky-headed teenager. The teenager looked sullen and in need of a wash. Rebus wondered if he were the man's son. If so, a lesson in parental control was definitely needed.
'Hi, Norman,' Penny Cook said in passing. The man smiled towards her. The teenager remained sullen: a controlled pose, Rebus decided. Further along, having passed through another combination-lock door, Penny herself cleared things up.
'Norman's one of our producers.'
'And the kid with him?'
'Kid?' She smiled wryly. 'That was Jez Jenks, the singer with Leftover Lunch. He probably makes more a day than you and I make in a good year.'
Rebus couldn't remember ever having a 'good year' – the curse of the honest copper. A question came to him.
'And Candy Barr?'

erübrigen • näherten sich

mit spitz abstehenden Haaren • mürrisch • elterlich

Kombinationsschloss

ironisch

Fluch • Bulle (Polizist) • (klingt wie „candy bar", Schokoriegel)

3. The spiky-haired teenager who was talking to a middle-aged man in the corridor was
- ☐ the singer of a band.
- ☐ one of the producers.
- ☐ the host of the station's afternoon show.

4. Inspector Rebus had come for an interview with Penny Cook because
- ☐ he was a big fan of hers.
- ☐ someone had broken into one of the offices.
- ☐ someone was threatening her.

wäre schwer zu übertreffen • Schauspielerin

She laughed at this. 'I thought my own name took some beating. Mind you, I don't suppose it's her real name. She's an actress or a comedienne or something. From across the water, of course.'

'Doesn't sound like an Irish name,' Rebus said as Penny Cook held open her office door.

engagiert

'I wouldn't make jokes around here, Inspector,' she said. 'You'll probably find yourself being signed up for a spot on one of our shows.'

(Varieté-Song) • schlug … vor • entsprechend

'The Laughing Policeman?' Rebus suggested. But then they were in the office, the door was closed, and the atmosphere cooled appropriately. This was business, after all. Serious business. She sat at her desk. Rebus sat down on the chair across from her.

'Do you want a coffee or anything, Inspector?'

'No thanks. So, when did these calls start, Miss Cook?'

tatsächlich • auf Sendung • tüchtig • Spaßanrufer

'About a month ago. The first time he tried it, he actually got through to me on-air. That takes some doing. The calls are filtered through two people before they get to me. Efficient people, too. They can usually tell a crank caller from the real thing.'

'How does the system work? Somebody calls in … then what?'

Übung 4 Kreuzen Sie den Begriff an, der nicht zu den anderen passt.

1. Which of the following things is <u>not</u> to be found in Penny Cook's office?

- ☐ a tape
- ☐ a phone box
- ☐ a ledge
- ☐ a desk

2. Which of the following expressions has nothing to do with telephoning?

- ☐ get through
- ☐ hold the line
- ☐ call in
- ☐ sign up

'Sue or David takes the call. They ask a few questions. Basically, they want to know the person's name, and what it is they want to talk to me about. Then they take a telephone number, tell the caller to stay by his or her telephone, and if we want to put the person on-air, they phone the caller back and prepare them.'

'Fairly rigorous then.'

'Oh yes. And even supposing the odd crank does get through, we've got a three-second delay on them when they're on-air. If they start cussing or raving, we cut the call before it goes out over the ether.'

'And is that what happened with this guy?'

'Pretty much.' She shook a cassette box at him. 'I've got the tape here. Do you want to hear?'

'Please.'

She started to load a cassette player on the ledge behind her. There were no windows in the office. From the number of steps they'd descended to get there, Rebus reckoned this whole floor of the building was located beneath ground-level.

'So you got a phone number for this guy?'

'Only it turned out to be a phone box in some housing scheme. We didn't know that at the time. We never

im Wesentlichen

gelegentlich • Spinner • Verzögerung • zu fluchen • zu toben

Band, Kassette

Ablage

die sie heruntergegangen waren • vermutete • unterhalb • stellte sich heraus • Wohnsiedlung

3. Which word does <u>not</u> refer to a person?

- a caller
- an actress
- a cassette player
- a copper

4. Which activity is <u>not</u> part of the call-in system at Lowland Radio?

- The calls are filtered.
- Penny takes all the calls.
- The callers must stay by their phones.
- There is a three-second delay.

5. Which of the following verbs is <u>not</u> a synonym of "think"?

- descend
- reckon
- suppose
- assume

usually take calls from phone boxes. But it was one of those ones that use the phone cards. No beeps, so nobody could tell.' She had loaded the tape to her satisfaction, but was now waiting for it to rewind. 'After he tried getting through again, we phoned his number. It rang and rang, and then some old girl picked it up. She explained where the box was. That was when we knew he'd tricked us.' The tape thumped to a stop. She hit the play button, and sat down again. There was hiss as the tape began, and then her voice filled the room. She smiled in embarrassment, as if to say: yes, it's a pose, this husky, sultry, late-night me. But it's a living …
'And now we've got Peter on line one. Peter, you're through to Penny Cook. How are things with you this evening?'
'Not so good, Penny.'
She interrupted the tape for a moment: 'This is where we cut him off.'
The man's voice had been sleepy, almost tranquillised. Now it erupted. 'I know what you're up to! I know what's going on!' The tape went dead. She leaned back in her chair and switched off the machine.
'It makes me shiver every time I hear it. That anger …

Pieptöne • dass es zurückspulte • kam mit einem dumpfen Geräusch zum Halten • Rauschen • verlegen • heißblütig • es hält mich über Wasser • hielt … an • wurde … laut • kam zum Stillstand • erschauern • Wut

Übung 5 Tragen Sie die gesuchten Begriffe in das Kreuzworträtsel ein.

1. frightened
2. to move your head up and down to show agreement
3. a small object that produces a flame
4. honest and friendly
5. a short high sound
6. to start suddenly
7. to stop someone or something from continuing
8. a strong negative feeling
9. to shake slightly because you are cold or frightened

such a sudden change in the voice. Brr.' She reached into her drawer and brought out cigarettes and lighter. Rebus accepted a cigarette from her.

plötzlich • Schublade • Feuerzeug

'Thanks,' he said. Then: 'The name'll be false, of course, but did he give a surname?'

Nachname

'A surname, an address, even a profession. He said he lived in Edinburgh, but we looked up the street name in the *A to Z* and it doesn't exist. From now on, we check that addresses are real before we call back. His surname was Gemmell. He even spelt it out for Sue. She couldn't believe he was a crank, he sounded so genuine.'

buchstabierte ihn • aufrichtig

'What did he tell her his problem was?'

'Drinking too much … how it was affecting his work. I like that sort of problem. The advice is straightforward, and it can be helping a lot of people too scared to phone in.'

sich auf … auswirkte • Rat • einfach • verängstigt

'What did he say his job was?'

'Bank executive. He gave Sue the bank's name and everything, and he kept saying it wasn't to be broadcast.' She smiled, shook her head. 'I mean, this nut really was *good*.'

Bankdirektor • Verrückter

Rebus nodded. 'He seems to have known the set-up pretty well.'

nickte • Ablauf

Schauplatz vieler Romane und Erzählungen von Ian Rankin:

1. ☐☐☐☐E☐
2. ☐☐D
3. ☐I☐☐☐☐☐
4. ☐☐☐☐☐N☐
5. B☐☐☐
6. ☐☐U☐
7. ☐☐☐☐☐R☐☐☐
8. ☐☐G☐
9. ☐H☐☐☐☐

ohne … auszulösen • gingen weiter • wir sind ihm auf die Schliche gekommen • dass er entdeckt worden ist

'You mean he got to the safe without triggering any of the alarms?' She smiled still. 'Oh yes, he's a real pro.'

'And the calls have persisted?'

'Most nights. We've got him tagged now though. He's tried using different accents … dialects … always a different name and job. But he hasn't managed to beat the system again. When he knows he's been found out, he does that whole routine again. "I know what you've done." Blah, blah. We put the phone down on him before he can get started.'

'And what *have* you done, Miss Cook?'

'Absolutely nothing, Inspector. Not that I know of.'

Rebus nodded slowly. 'Can I hear the tape again?'

spulte

'Sure.' She wound it back, and they listened together. Then she excused herself – 'to powder my nose' – and Rebus listened twice more. When she returned, she was carrying two plastic beakers of coffee.

Becher • in Versuchung führen

'Thought I might tempt you,' she said. 'Milk, no sugar … I hope that's all right.'

'Thank you, yes, that's just the job.'

'So, Inspector, what do you think?'

nippte an • lauwarm • Flüssigkeit

He sipped the lukewarm liquid. 'I think,' he said, 'you've got an anonymous phone-caller.'

Übung 6

Welche Satzteile passen zusammen?
Tragen Sie die entsprechenden Buchstaben in die Kästchen ein.

1. ☐ The crank caller tried to get through to Penny almost every night

2. ☐ When the anonymous caller knew that he had been found out, he shouted "I know what you've done!".

3. ☐ If they wanted to trace the caller,

4. ☐ While the inspector was listening to the tape again,

5. ☐ Penny told Inspector Rebus that she did not make enemies

6. ☐ Rebus suggested that other radio stations might be jealous of Penny's ratings,

She raised her cup, as though to toast him. 'God bless CID,' she said. 'What would we do without you?'
'The problem is that he's probably mobile, not sticking to the same telephone kiosk every time. That's supposing he's as clever as he seems. We can get BT to put a trace on him, but for that you'd have to keep him talking. Or, if he gives his number, we can trace him from that. But it takes time.'
'And meanwhile he could be slipping off into the night?'
'I'm afraid so. Still, apart from continuing to fend him off and hoping he gets fed up, I can't see what else can be done. You don't recognise the voice? Someone from your past ... an ex-lover ... someone with a grudge?'
'I don't make enemies, Inspector.'
Looking at her, listening to her voice, he found that easy to believe. Maybe not personal enemies ...
'What about the other radio stations? They can't be too thrilled about your ratings.'
Her laughter was loud. 'You think they've put out a contract on me, is that it?'
Rebus smiled and shrugged. 'Just a thought. But yours *is* the most popular show Lowland has got, isn't it?'

hob • als ob sie auf ihn trinken wollte • Kriminalpolizei • vorausgesetzt • British Telecom • seine Anrufe zurückzuverfolgen • entwischen

ihn abzuwehren • dass er die Lust verliert • der eine alte Rechnung zu begleichen hat

begeistert • Einschaltquoten • jemanden auf mich angesetzt • zuckte mit den Schultern

a) and, looking at her and listening to her voice, he found that easy to believe.
b) Penny Cook had no idea what he might be referring to.
c) but she just laughed at the idea that one of them might have hired someone to make the calls.
d) using different accents and dialects and giving different names and jobs.
e) they had to keep him talking for some time.
f) Penny got two cups of coffee.

vor • 'I think I'm still just about ahead of Hamish, yes. But then Hamish's show is just ... well, Hamish. My show's all about the people themselves, the ones who call in. Human interest, you could say.'

'And there's plenty of interest.'

Leid • zieht ... an • ein bisschen • verstört • und ich tue so, als ob • reumütig

'Suffering is always interesting, isn't it? It appeals to the voyeur. We *do* get our fair share of crank calls. Maybe that's why. All those lonely, slightly deranged people out there ... listening to me. Me, pretending I've got all the answers.' Her smile this time was rueful. 'The calls recently have been getting ... I don't know whether to say "better" or "worse". Worse problems, better radio.'

'Better for your ratings, you mean?'

Werbekunden • allgemein bekannt • fielen schon etwas zurück • Marktforschung • umfasste • aufzustehen

'Most advertisers ignore the late-night slots. That's common knowledge. Not a big enough audience. But it's never been a problem on my show. We did slip back for a little while, but the figures picked up again. Up and up and up ... Don't ask me what sort of listeners we're attracting. I leave all that to market research.' Rebus finished his coffee and clasped both knees, preparing to rise. 'I'd like to take the tape with me, is that possible?'

Übung 7

Vervollständigen Sie die folgenden Sätze mit dem passenden Wort. (pretending, ejected, problems, ahead of, maze, night shift, fan mail, market research)

1. Inspector Rebus couldn't talk to Sue. She was not in yet, because she was on ______________ today.

2. As far as the ratings were concerned, Penny was still ______________ Hamish.

3. Penny Cook's show was mainly about the people who called in and about their ______________.

'Sure.' She ejected the tape. — warf … aus

'And I'd like to have a word with … Sue, is it?'

She checked her watch. 'Sue, yes, but she won't be in for a few hours yet. Night shift, you see. Only us poor disc jockeys have to be here twenty-four hours. I exaggerate, but it feels like it sometimes.' She patted a tray on the ledge beside the cassette player. The tray was filled with correspondence. 'Besides, I have my fan mail to deal with.'

Rebus nodded, glanced at the cassette tape he was now holding. 'Let me have a think about this, Miss Cook. I'll see what we can do.'

'OK, Inspector.'

'Sorry I can't be more constructive. You were quite right to contact us.'

'I didn't suppose there was much you could – '

'We don't know that yet. As I say, give me a little time to think about it.'

She rose from her chair. 'I'll see you out. This place is a maze, and we can't have you stumbling in on the *Afternoon Show*, can we? You might end up doing your Laughing Policeman routine after all …'

Nachtschicht • übertreibe • tätschelte • Korb

um die ich mich kümmern muss • warf einen Blick

ich habe nicht angenommen

erhob sich • Labyrinth • hineinstolpern

4. Penny admitted that she was only ____________________ to have all the right answers to her callers' problems.

5. In order to find out what age groups listen to their shows radio stations have to do ____________________.

6. Inspector Rebus wanted to take the tape with him, so Penny ____________________ it.

7. The building was like a ____________________ – there were so many corridors and doors that you could easily get lost.

8. Apart from hosting her show Penny had to answer piles of ____________________.

gedämpft • Treppenhaus • pummelig • zerzaust • stark gerötet • deutlich • geschniegelt • aufgewogen • mit Paisleymuster • zwei Fliegen mit einer Klappe zu schlagen • berüchtigt

As they were walking down the long, hushed corridor, Rebus saw two men in conversation at the bottom of the stairwell. One was a beefy, hearty-looking man with a mass of rumpled hair and a good growth of beard. His cheeks seemed veined with blood. The other man proved a significant contrast, small and thin with slicked-back hair. He wore a grey suit and white shirt, the latter offset by a bright red paisley-patterned tie.

'Ah,' said Penny Cook quietly, 'a chance to kill two birds. Come on, let me introduce you to Gordon Prentice – he's the station chief – and to the infamous Hamish MacDiarmid.'

völlig • schüttelte ihm die Hand fast ab

Well, Rebus had no trouble deciding which man was which. Except that, when Penny did make the introductions, he was proved utterly wrong. The bearded man pumped his hand.

ausgebeult • hervorquollen • drahtig • schlaff • Speiseschrank

'I hope you're going to be able to help, Inspector. There are some sick minds out there.' This was Gordon Prentice. He wore baggy brown cords and an open-necked shirt from which protruded tufts of wiry hair. Hamish MacDiarmid's hand, when Rebus took it, was limp and cool, like something lifted from a larder. No matter how hard he tried, Rebus couldn't match this … for

Übung 8 Sind die folgenden Aussagen wahr oder falsch?
Tragen Sie ein T für true oder ein F für false in die Kästchen ein.

1. There was a lot of noise in the corridor when Inspector Rebus and Penny left the office.
2. Penny introduced Inspector Rebus to her boss and to Hamish MacDiarmid.
3. Hamish MacDiarmid looked just as Inspector Rebus had expected.
4. Gordon Prentice – Penny's boss – wore a grey suit and white shirt.

want of a better word, *yuppie* … couldn't match him to the combative voice. But then MacDiarmid spoke.
'Sick minds is right, and stupid minds too. I don't know which is worse, a deranged audience or an educationally subnormal one.' He turned to Penny Cook. 'Maybe you got the better bargain, Penelope.' He turned back to Prentice. So that's what a sneer looks like, Rebus thought. But MacDiarmid was speaking again. 'Gordon, how about letting Penny and me swap shows for a day? She could sit there agreeing with every bigoted caller I get, and I could get stuck in about her social cripples. What do you think?'
Prentice chuckled and placed a hand on the shoulder of both his star DJs. 'I'll give it some thought, Hamish. Penny might not be too thrilled though. I think she has a soft spot for her "cripples".'

in Einklang bringen mit • streitlustig

Geschäft • Spötter

tauschen

selbstgerecht • Krüppel • schmunzelte

nicht gerade erpicht • Schwäche

Penny Cook certainly didn't look 'too thrilled' by the time Rebus and she were out of earshot.
'Those two,' she hissed. 'Sometimes they act like I'm not even there! Men …' She glanced towards Rebus. 'Present company excluded, of course.'
'I'll take that as a compliment.'

außer Hörweite • zischte

Anwesende ausgenommen

5. Gordon was a healthy-looking, rather plump man with a beard and a mass of hair on his head.
6. Gordon Prentice had a very firm grip, whereas MacDiarmid's handshake was rather weak.
7. MacDiarmid suggested to Gordon Prentice that Penny should do his show for one day and vice versa.
8. Penny liked the idea of swapping shows with MacDiarmid.
9. MacDiarmid sneered at Penny's audience and called them "social cripples".
10. Penny hated it when MacDiarmid and Gordon Prentice seemed to ignore her.

so gemein sein zu
'I shouldn't be so hard on Gordon actually. I know I joke about being here twenty-four hours a day, but I really think he *does* spend all day and all night at the station. He's here from early morning, but each night he comes into the studio to listen to a bit of my show. Beyond the call of duty, wouldn't you say?'

weit mehr als nur Pflichterfüllung • bloß • wette

Rebus merely shrugged.

'I bet,' she went on, 'when you saw them you thought it was Hamish with the beard.'

PR-Fotos

Rebus nodded. She giggled. 'Everybody does,' she said. 'Nobody's what they seem in this place. I'll let you into a secret. The station doesn't keep any publicity shots of Hamish. They're afraid it would hurt his image if everyone found out he looks like a wimp.'

Schwächling, Weichei • ganz • mehrdeutig

'He's certainly not *quite* what I expected.'

She gave him an ambiguous look. 'No, well, *you're* not quite what *I* was expecting either.' There was a moment's stillness between them, broken only by some coffee commercial being broadcast from the ceiling: '... but Camelot Coffee is no myth, and mmm ... it tastes *so* good.' They smiled at one another and walked on.

Werbespot

Übung 9 Vervollständigen Sie die Ausdrücke, indem Sie den fehlenden Teil ergänzen. Die folgende Wortauswahl soll Ihnen dabei helfen:
(a fifty-pence, of duty, an ambiguous, gimmick, of coffee, publicity)

1. ________________ shots
2. the call ________________
3. ________________ refund
4. a jar ________________
5. a promotional ________________
6. ________________ look

Driving back into Edinburgh, Rebus listened, despite himself, to the drivel on Lowland Radio. Advertising was tight, he knew that. Maybe that was why he seemed to hear the same dozen or so adverts over and over again. Lots of air-time to fill and so few advertisers to fill it … '… and mmm … it tastes *so* good.'
That particular advert was beginning to get to him. It careered around in his head, even when it wasn't being broadcast. The actor's voice was so … what was the word? It was like being force-fed a tablespoon of honey. Cloying, sickly, altogether too much.
'Was Camelot* a myth or is it real? Arthur* and Guinevere*, Merlin* and Lancelot*. A dream, or – '
Rebus switched off the radio. 'It's only a jar of bloody coffee,' he told his radio set. Yes, he thought, a jar of coffee … and mmm … it tastes *so* good. Come to think of it, he needed coffee for the flat. He'd stop off at the corner shop, and whatever he bought it wouldn't be Camelot.

widerwillig • Gefasel • knapp • Dutzend • Werbespots • wenige • ihm auf den Geist zu gehen • raste • zwangsweise verabreicht • übermäßig süß • widerlich • Glas

But, as a promotional gimmick, there was a fifty-pence refund on Camelot, so Rebus did buy it, and sat at home that evening drinking the vile stuff and listening

Werbegag • Rückerstattung • widerwärtig

info

Der sagenumwobene König Artus (King Arthur), König von England und Wales, soll im 5. Jahrhundert n. Chr. mit seiner Frau Guinevere in Camelot residiert haben. Wo sich Camelot genau befand, ist bis heute nicht geklärt. Überreste von verschiedenen Burgen in Wales und England haben die Vermutung nahegelegt, dass es sich um Camelot handeln könnte.
Am Hof von Camelot versammelte König Artus seine Ritter an einem runden Tisch, um keine Rangstreitigkeiten aufkommen zu lassen. Lancelot war einer der Ritter der Tafelrunde.
Der Magier Merlin soll das berühmte Schwert Excalibur in einen Stein gesteckt haben, aus dem es nur vom wahren König – Artus – herausgezogen werden konnte.

to Penny Cook's tape. Tomorrow evening, he was thinking, he might go along to the station to catch her show live. He had an excuse after all: he wanted to speak with Sue, the telephonist. That was the excuse; the truth was that he was intrigued by Penny Cook herself. *You're not quite what I was expecting.*

Was he reading too much into that one sentence? Maybe he was. Well, put it another way then: he had a *duty* to return to Lowland Radio, a duty to talk to Sue. He wound the tape back for the umpteenth time. That ferocious voice. Sue had been surprised by its ferocity, hadn't she? The man had seemed so quiet, so polite in their initial conversation. Rebus was stuck. Maybe the caller *would* simply get fed up. When it was a question of someone's home being called, there were steps you could take: have someone intercept all calls, change the person's number and keep it ex-directory. But Penny Cook needed her number to be public. She couldn't hide, except behind the wall provided by Sue and David. Then he had an idea. It wasn't much of an idea, but it was better than nothing. Bill Costain at the Forensic Science Lab was keen on sound recording, tape recorders, all that sort of stuff. Maybe he could do

Vorwand
fasziniert
Verpflichtung • zum x-ten Mal • wütend
steckte fest
abhören • nicht im Telefonbuch eingetragen • (dar)gestellt von • kriminaltechnisches Labor • scharf auf

Übung 10 Welche der angegebenen Möglichkeiten ist die richtige? Kreuzen Sie sie an.

1. Inspector Rebus was going to listen to Penny's show live at the radio station
- ☐ after he had solved the case.
- ☐ that night.
- ☐ the following evening.

2. If people want to make sure that no unwanted caller rings them,
- ☐ they can simply not answer the phone.
- ☐ they can keep their phone number ex-directory.
- ☐ they should get a new phone number every few months.

something with Mr Anonymous. Yes, he'd call him first thing tomorrow. He sipped his coffee, then squirmed. 'Tastes more like camel than Camelot,' he muttered, hitting the play button.

schauderte • brummelte

The morning was bright and clear, but Bill Costain was dull and overcast.
'I was playing in a darts match last night,' he explained. 'We won for a change. The amount of drink we put away, you'd think Scotland had just done the Grand Slam.'
'Never mind,' said Rebus, handing over the cassette tape. 'I've brought you something soothing …'
'Soothing' wasn't the word Costain himself used after listening to the tape. But he enjoyed a challenge, and the challenge Rebus had laid down was to tell him anything at all about the voice. He listened several times to the tape, and put it through some sort of analyser, the voice becoming a series of peaks and troughs.
Costain scratched his head. 'There's too big a difference between the voice at the beginning and the voice when hysterical.' 'How do you mean?' Costain always seemed able to baffle Rebus.

grau • trüb(sinnig) • zur Abwechslung • alle Gegner im Rugby-Turnier Six Nations besiegt

Herausforderung • gestellt hatte

Spitzen • Tiefen • kratzte

verblüffen

3. Inspector Rebus went to see someone who could
- ☐ intercept all the phone calls that were made to Penny Cook at the radio station.
- ☐ analyse the sound recording.
- ☐ make a chemical analysis of Camelot coffee.

4. Bill Costain didn't look and feel very well that morning because
- ☐ he had lost a darts match the night before.
- ☐ he had eaten too many sausages for breakfast.
- ☐ he had celebrated his team's victory in a darts match the night before and had drunk too much alcohol.

'The hysterical voice is so much higher than the voice at the beginning. It's hardly … natural.'
'Meaning?'
'I'd say one of them's a put-on. Probably the initial voice. He's disguising his normal tone, speaking in a lower register than usual.'
'So can we get back to his *real* voice?'
'You mean can we retrieve it? Yes, but the lab isn't the best place for that. A friend of mine has a recording studio out Morningside* way. I'll give him a bell …'
They were in luck. The studio's facilities were not in use that morning. Rebus drove them to Morningside and then sat back as Costain and his friend got busy at the mixing console. They slowed the hysteric part of the tape; then managed somehow to take the pitch of the voice down several tones. It began to sound more than slightly unnatural, like a Dalek* or something electronic. But then they started to build it back up again, until Rebus was listening to a slow, almost lifeless vocal over the studio's huge monitor speakers.
'I … know … what … you've … done.'
Yes, there was life there now, almost a hint of personality. After this, they switched to the caller's first utter-

kaum • Und das bedeutet? • verstellt • verschleiert • Tonlage • herausbekommen • ihn anrufen • Anlage • schafften es • Tonhöhe • Hauch • Äußerung

info

Morningside ist ein im Südwesten gelegener Stadtteil Edinburghs. Dort finden sich neben größeren Wohnanlagen auch eine Reihe alter viktorianischer Villen. Bei Studenten ist diese Gegend wegen ihrer Nähe zur Universität sehr beliebt, gilt aber auch als sehr versnobt.

Daleks sind außerirdische, roboterähnliche Mutanten, die in der britischen TV-Serie Doctor Who die Erde bedrohen.
Mit schriller, elektronischer Stimme geben sie regelmäßig ihren Lieblings-Slogan zum Besten: „EX-TER-MI-NATE!“

ance – 'Not so good, Penny' – and played around with it, heightening the pitch slightly, even speeding it up a bit.
'That's about as good as it gets,' Costain said at last.
'It's brilliant, Bill, thanks. Can I get a copy?'
Having dropped Costain back at the lab, Rebus wormed his way back through the lunchtime traffic to Great London Road police station. He played this new tape several times, then switched from tape to radio. Christ, he'd forgotten: it was still tuned to Lowland.
'... and mmm ... it tastes *so* good.'
Rebus fairly growled as he reached for the off button. But the damage, the delirious, wonderful damage, had already been done ...

erhöhten • beschleunigten

Nachdem er ... abgesetzt hatte • schlängelte sich

auf ... eingestellt

geradezu • knurrte

The wine bar was on the corner of Hanover Street and Queen Street. It was a typical Edinburgh affair in that though it might have started with wine, quiche and salad in mind, it had reverted to beer – albeit mainly of the 'designer' variety – and pies. Always supposing you could call something filled with chickpeas and spices a 'pie'. Still, it had an IPA pump, and that was good enough for Rebus. The place had just finished its

Sache • zu ... zurückgekehrt war • wenn auch • Kichererbsen • Gewürze • (Biermarke)

Übung 11

Bringen Sie die Buchstaben der Wörter in Klammern in die richtige Reihenfolge und vervollständigen Sie dann die folgenden Sätze.

1. The anonymous caller was ________________ (gsiunsigid) his voice by speaking in a lower tone.

2. Inspector Rebus and Bill Costain used the ________________ (ticfealisi) of a recording studio to retrieve the caller's real voice.

3. The radio at Rebus's office was still ________________ (netdu) to Lowland Radio.

4. Rebus ________________ (lowderg) when he heard the Camelot commercial again.

lunchtime peak, and tables were still cluttered with plates, glasses and condiments. Having paid over the odds for his drink, Rebus felt the barman owed him a favour. He gave the young man a name. The barman nodded towards a table near the window. The table's sole occupant looked just out of his teens. He flicked a lock of hair back from his forehead and gazed out of the window. There was a newspaper folded into quarters on his knee. He tapped his teeth with a ballpoint, mulling over some crossword clue. Without asking, Rebus sat down opposite him. 'It whiles away the time,' he said. The tooth-tapper seemed still intent on the window. Maybe he could see his reflection there. The modern Narcissus. Another flick of the hair.

'If you got a haircut, you wouldn't need to keep doing that.'

This achieved a smile. Maybe he thought Rebus was trying to chat him up. Well, after all, this was known as an actors' bar, wasn't it? Half a glass of orange juice sat on the table, the ubiquitous ice-cube having melted away to a sliver.

'Aye,' Rebus mused, 'passes the time.'

This time the eyes turned from the window and were

Stoßzeit • überhäuft • Würzmittel • zu viel • schuldete ihm einen Gefallen • einzige Gast • strich sich

tippte gegen • und grübelte • Kreuzworträtselfrage • vertreibt • konzentriert auf

brachte … hervor

unvermeidlich • Scheibchen • ja

Übung 12 Welche Form ist die richtige – Adjektiv oder Adverb?

1. After the lunchtime peak the pub became a ______________ (quiet/quietly) place.
2. The barman ______________ (careful/carefully) put the glasses onto the shelf behind the bar.
3. Rebus finished his drink ______________ (quick/quickly).
4. The young man was sitting at the table, ______________ (quiet/quietly) doing a crossword puzzle.
5. The ice-cube was ______________ (slow/slowly) melting away in the glass of orange juice.

on him. Rebus leaned forward across the table. When he spoke, he spoke quietly, confidently. — selbstsicher

'I know what you've done,' he said, not sure even as he said it whether he were quoting or speaking for himself. — zitierte

The lock of hair fell forward and stayed there. A frozen second, then another, and the man rose quickly to his feet, the chair tipping back. But Rebus, still seated, had grabbed at an arm and held it fast. — wie eingefroren • wobei … nach hinten kippte

'Let go of me!'

'Sit down.'

'I said let go!'

'And I said sit down!' Rebus pulled him back on to his chair. 'That's better. We've got a lot to talk about, you and me. We can do it here or down at the station, and by "station" I don't mean Scotrail. OK?' — (schottische Bahngesellschaft)

The head was bowed, the careful hair now almost completely dishevelled. It was that easy … Rebus found the tiniest grain of pity. 'Do you want something else to drink?' The head shook from side to side. 'Not even a cup of coffee?' — • gesenkt • zerzaust • winzigste Quäntchen Mitleid

Now the head looked up at him.

'I saw the film once,' Rebus went on. 'Bloody awful it

6. Rebus's voice was ______________ (confident/confidently) when he said: "I know what you've done."

7. As the man looked at Rebus ______________ (nervous/nervously), the lock of hair fell forward again.

8. He threw a ______________ (quick/quickly) glance towards the door.

9. Rebus, who had obviously expected a ______________ (sudden/suddenly) movement, grabbed the young man's arm and pulled him back.

10. "Sit down ______________ (immediate/immediately)!" Rebus ordered.

was, but not half as bad as the coffee. Give me Richard Harris's* singing any day.'

grinste • den Ausdruck entschuldigen • zu plaudern (wörtl. die Bohnen auszuschütten; Anspielung auf den Kaffee)

Now, finally, the head grinned. 'That's better,' said Rebus. 'Come on, son. It's time, if you'll pardon the expression, to spill the beans.'
The beans spilled …

Rebus was there that night for *What's Cookin'*. It surprised him that Penny Cook herself, who sounded so calm on the air, was, before the programme, a complete bundle of nerves. She slipped a small yellow tablet on to her tongue and washed it down with a beaker of water.

naheliegend

'Don't ask,' she said, cutting off the obvious question. Sue and David were stationed by their telephones in the production room; which was separated from Penny's studio by a large glass window. Her producer did his best to calm things down. Though not yet out of his thirties, he looked to be an old pro at this. Rebus wondered if he shouldn't have his own counselling show … Rebus chatted with Sue for ten minutes or so, and watched as the production team went through its paces. Really, it was a two-man operation – producer

abgetrennt • Profi • Beratungs- • Schritte

info

Richard Harris, 1930 im irischen Limerick geboren, spielte und sang den Part von König Artus in der Kinoversion des Broadway-Stücks Camelot – deshalb Inspector Rebus' Anspielung auf den Kaffee gleichen Namens. In seiner letzten großen Rolle war Harris in der Verfilmung der ersten beiden Harry-Potter-Bände als Professor Albus Dumbledore zu sehen.

Keep your fingers crossed lässt sich im Deutschen mit „Drück mir die Daumen!" wiedergeben. Der Ausdruck geht auf die Vorstellung zurück, dass mit dem Zeichen des Kreuzes Unglück ferngehalten werden könne.

and engineer. There was a last-minute panic when Penny's microphone started to play up, but the engineer was swift to replace it. By five minutes to eleven, the hysteria seemed over. Everyone was calm now, or was so tense it didn't show. Like troops just before a battle, Rebus was thinking. Penny had a couple of questions about the running order of the night's musical pieces. She held a conversation with her producer, communicating via mikes and headphones, but looking at one another through the window.

Then she turned her eyes towards Rebus, winked at him, and crossed her fingers*.

He crossed his fingers back at her.

'Two minutes everyone ...'

At the top of the hour there was news, and straight after the news ...

A tape played. The show's theme music. Penny leaned towards her microphone, which hung like an anglepoise over her desk. The music faded.

'Hello again. This is Penny Cook, and this is *What's Cookin'*. I'll be with you until three o'clock, so if you've got a problem, I'm just a phone call away. And if you want to ring me the number as ever is ...'

Techniker • verrückt zu spielen • schnell

angespannt • Schlacht

Mikrofone

zwinkerte ... zu

Gelenkleuchte • wurde leiser

Übung 13

Bringen Sie die Aussagen in die richtige Reihenfolge und tragen Sie die entsprechenden Nummern in die Kästchen ein.

- [1] Before her show Penny was a complete bundle of nerves.
- [ ] After the news the show's theme music was played.
- [ ] Penny wanted to know the order in which the musical pieces would be played.
- [ ] The production team went through its paces.
- [ ] She winked at Inspector Rebus and crossed her fingers.
- [ ] She swallowed a small yellow tablet.
- [ ] The music faded and Penny went on the air.
- [ ] Penny's microphone had to be replaced.

darüber staunen • zerbrechlich • getrennt von • besäße • war er doch lieber • Uhrwerk • geeignet • Zwischenprogramm • Einwände erheben • Ehebruch

It was extraordinary, and Rebus could only marvel at it. Her eyes were closed, and she looked so brittle that a shiver might turn her to powder. Yet that voice ... so controlled ... no, not controlled; rather, it was as though it were apart from her, as though it possessed a life of its own, a personality ... Rebus looked at the studio clock. Four hours of this, five nights a week? All in all, he thought, he'd rather be a policeman.

The show was running like clockwork. Calls were taken by the two operators, details scribbled down. There was discussion with the producer about suitable candidates, and during the musical interludes or the commercials – '... and mmm ... it tastes *so* good' – the producer would relay details about the callers to Penny.

'Let's go with that one,' she might say. Or: 'I can't deal with that, not tonight.' Usually, her word was the last, though the producer might demur.

'I don't know, it's quite a while since we covered adultery ...'

Rebus watched. Rebus listened. But most of all, Rebus waited ...

'OK, Penny,' the producer told her, 'it's line two next. His name's Michael.'

Übung 14 Setzen Sie die passenden Präpositionen in die Lücken ein: (about, at, on, into, through, from, down)

1. At quarter to midnight Gordon Prentice came ____________ the room.
2. Penny's voice sounded as if it was apart ____________ her.
3. Inspector Rebus looked ____________ her ____________ the large glass window.
4. The two operators scribbled ____________ details ____________ the callers.
5. "And now we've got Michael ____________ line two." Penny said.

She nodded. 'Can somebody get me a coffee?'
'Sure.'
'And next,' she said, 'I think we've got Michael on line two. Hello, Michael?'
It was quarter to midnight. As usual, the door of the production room opened and Gordon Prentice stepped into the room. He had nods and smiles for everyone, and seemed especially pleased to see Rebus.
'Inspector,' he said shaking Rebus's hand. 'I see you take your work seriously, coming here at this hour.' He patted the producer's shoulder. 'How's the show tonight?'
'Been a bit tame so far, but this looks interesting.'
Penny's eyes were on the dimly lit production room. But her voice was all for Michael.
'And what do you do for a living, Michael?'
The caller's voice crackled out of the loudspeakers. 'I'm an actor, Penny.'
'Really? And are you working just now?'
'No, I'm what we call "resting".'
'Ah well, they say there's no rest for the wicked. I suppose that must mean you *haven't* been wicked.'
Gordon Prentice, running his fingers through his

erfreut

lahm • schwach beleuchtet

knisterte

ohne Engagement • Pause, Ruhe • die Bösen

Welches Wort kann nicht wie die anderen durch Anhängen von -able oder -ion die Wortart wechseln?

Übung 15

1. agree, suit, smile, read — -able

2. discuss, work, protect, possess — -ion

beard, smiled at this, turning to Rebus to see how he was enjoying himself. Rebus smiled back.
'On the contrary,' the voice was saying. 'I've been really quite wicked. And I'm ashamed of it.'
'And what is it you're so ashamed of, Michael?'
'I've been telephoning you anonymously, Penny. Threatening you. I'm sorry. You see, I thought you knew about it. But the policeman tells me you don't. I'm sorry.' Prentice wasn't smiling now. His eyes had opened wide in disbelief.
'Knew about what, Michael?' Her eyes were staring at the window. Light bounced off her spectacles, sending flashes like laser beams into the production room.
'Knew about the fix. When the ratings were going down, the station head, Gordon Prentice, started rigging the shows, yours and Hamish MacDiarmid's. MacDiarmid might even be in on it.'
'What do you mean, rigging?'
'Kill it!' shouted Prentice. 'Kill transmission! He's raving mad! Cut the line someone. Here, I'll do it – '
But Rebus had come up behind Prentice and now locked his own arms around Prentice's. 'I think you'd better listen,' he warned.

im Gegenteil • ich schäme mich • ungläubig • reflektierte • Brille • Blitze • Strahlen • abgekartetes Spiel • zu manipulieren • total verrückt • packte ... mit den Armen

Übung 16 Lösen Sie das Kreuzworträtsel mithilfe der folgenden Erklärungen:

Down ↓

1 feeling really bad because of something you have done
2 the opposite of what has been said or suggested
3 a shining line of light

Across →

4 They help you to see clearly.
5 all the actors in a film or play
6 to shout something very loudly

'Out of work actors,' Michael was saying, the way he'd told Rebus earlier in the day. 'Prentice put together a … you could call it a cast, I suppose. Half a dozen people. They phone in using different voices, always with a controversial point to make or some nice juicy problem. One of them told me at a party one night. I didn't believe her until I started listening for myself. An actor can tell that sort of thing, when a voice isn't quite right, when something's an act rather than for real.'

Prentice was struggling, but couldn't break Rebus's hold. 'Lies!' he yelled. 'Complete rubbish! Let go of me, you – '

Penny Cook's eyes were on Prentice now, and on no one but Prentice.

'So what you're saying, Michael, if I understand you, is that Gordon Prentice is rigging our phone-ins so as to boost audience figures?'

'That's right.'

'Michael, thank you for your call.'

It was Rebus who spoke, and he spoke to the producer. 'That'll do.'

The producer nodded through the glass to Penny

out of work – arbeitslos
cast – Besetzung
juicy – interessant
was struggling – wehrte sich
yelled – schrie
as to boost – um … zu steigern

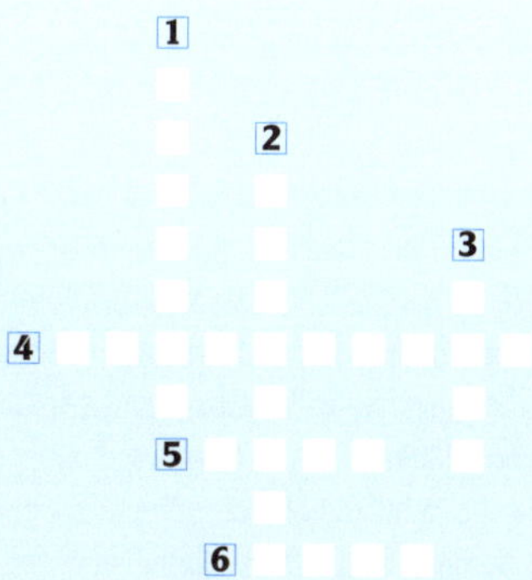

legte einen Schalter um	Cook, then flipped a switch. Music could be heard over the loudspeakers. The producer started to fade the piece out. Penny spoke into her microphone.
	'A slightly longer musical interlude there, but I hope you enjoyed it. We'll be going back to your calls very shortly, but first we've got some commercials.'
zog herunter • ihren Nasenrücken •	She slipped off her glasses and rubbed the bridge of her nose.
Nur für uns.	'A private performance,' Rebus explained to Prentice. 'For our benefit only. The listeners were hearing something else.' Rebus felt Prentice's body soften, the shoulders slump. He was caught, and knew it for sure. Rebus relaxed his hold on the man: he wouldn't try anything now.
als er … erkannt hatte • die beteiligt war • der betroffen war	The Camelot Coffee ad was playing. It had been easy really. Recognising the voice on the commercial as that of the phone caller, Rebus had contacted the ad agency involved, who had given him the name and address of the actor concerned: Michael Barrie, presently resting and to be found most days in a certain city-centre wine bar …
	Barrie knew he was in trouble, but Rebus was sure it could be smoothed out. But as for Gordon Prentice …

Übung 17 Welche Satzteile passen zusammen?
Tragen Sie den entsprechenden Buchstaben in die Kästchen ein.

1. ☐ When Inspector Rebus had listened to the Camelot coffee commercial once more,
2. ☐ In order to get the actor's name and address
3. ☐ The young man Rebus had questioned at the wine bar
4. ☐ When Michael had called Penny at the station and threatened her,
5. ☐ Penny shot a baleful glance in Prentice's direction,
6. ☐ After Gordon Prentice's manipulation of the phone-ins was discovered,

ah, that was different altogether.
'The station's ruined!' he wailed. 'You must know that!' He pleaded with the producer, the engineer, but especially with the hate-filled eyes of Penny Cook who, behind glass, could not even hear him. 'Once this gets out, you'll *all* be out of a job! All of you! That's why I – '
'Back on in five seconds, Penny,' said the producer, as though it was just another night on *What's Cookin'*. Penny Cook nodded, resting her glasses back on her nose. The stuffing looked to have been knocked out of her. With one final baleful glance towards Prentice, she turned to her microphone.
'Welcome back. A change of direction now, because I'd like to say a few words to you about the head of Lowland Radio, Gordon Prentice. I hope you'll bear with me for a minute or two. It shouldn't take much longer than that …'

jammerte • flehte inständig

als ob

Innenleben • unheilvoll

sich … gedulden

It didn't, but what she said was tabloid news by morning, and Lowland Radio's licence was withdrawn not long after that. Rebus went back to Radio Three for when he was driving, and no radio at all in his flat. Hamish MacDiarmid, as far as he could ascertain, went

Boulevardpresse • entzogen

herausfinden

a) the radio station lost its licence and Penny Cook and Hamish MacDiarmid lost their jobs.
b) he had suddenly realised that the voice of the man in the commercial and the voice of the anonymous caller were identical.
c) was Michael Barrie, an out-of-work actor.
d) before she told her listeners about what he had done.
e) he had thought that she knew about Gordon Prentice's plan.
f) Rebus had contacted the ad agency.

Cottage in den Highlands • arbeitete freiberuflich

back to a croft somewhere, but Penny Cook stuck around, going freelance and doing some journalism as well as the odd radio programme.

It was very late one night when the knock came at Rebus's door. He opened it to find Penny standing there. She pretended surprise at seeing him.

mir ist der Kaffee ausgegangen

'Oh, hello,' she said. 'I didn't know you lived here. Only, I've run out of coffee and I was wondering …'

Laughing, Rebus led her inside. 'I can let you have the best part of a jar of Camelot,' he said. 'Or alternatively we could get drunk and go to bed …'

They got drunk.

Übung 18 Die folgenden Dinge haben eines gemeinsam – sie alle haben einen Rücken. Wie lauten die entsprechenden englischen Begriffe? Schreiben Sie die richtigen Buchstaben in die Kästchen.

a ridge b bridge c spine d back

☐ Nasenrücken
☐ Buchrücken
☐ Handrücken
☐ Bergrücken

Castle Dangerous

AN INSPECTOR REBUS STORY

Sir Walter Scott* was dead.
He'd been found at the top of his namesake's monument in Princes Street Gardens, dead of a heart attack and with a new and powerful pair of binoculars hanging around his slender, mottled neck.
Sir Walter had been one of Edinburgh's most revered QCs until his retirement a year ago. Detective Inspector John Rebus, climbing the hundreds (surely it must be hundreds) of spiralling steps up to the top of the Scott Monument, paused for a moment to recall one or two of his run-ins with Sir Walter, both in and out of the courtrooms on the Royal Mile*. He had been a formidable character, shrewd, devious and subtle. Law to him had been a challenge rather than an obligation. To John Rebus, it was just a day's work.

Namensvetter • Herzinfarkt • Fernglas • schmal • fleckig • Hals • verehrt • Kronanwälte • Pensionierung • spiralförmig gewunden • um sich … ins Gedächtnis zu rufen • Gerichtssäle • scharfsinnig • verschlagen • Pflicht

info

Der berühmte Namensvetter, Sir Walter Scott, gilt als einer der bedeutendsten Schriftsteller Großbritanniens. Er wurde 1771 als Walter Scott in Edinburgh geboren. Nach dem Jurastudium wurde er wie sein Vater Anwalt, verfasste aber nebenbei Gedichte und schrieb als Erster in Großbritannien historische Romane. Viele seiner Werke, wie zum Beispiel Waverley und Ivanhoe, wurden zu Klassikern der Literatur. In Anerkennung seiner Verdienste wurde er als Baronet in den Adelsstand erhoben und erhielt den Titel Sir Walter Scott.

Die Royal Mile, ein geschichtsträchtiger Straßenzug, führt vom Fuß des Stadtbergs Arthur's Seat bis zum Castle durch die Edinburgher Altstadt.

tat alles weh • Anstieg • enger • Gipfel • Gedränge • die sich … quetschten • furchterregend • atmete • als er sich … zwängte • Aussicht • ausgebreitet • abfallend • erkennbar	Rebus ached as he reached the last incline. The steps here were narrower than ever, the spiral tighter. Room for one person only, really. At the height of its summer popularity, with a throng of tourists squeezing through it like toothpaste from a tube, Rebus reckoned the Scott Monument might be very scary indeed. He breathed hard and loud, bursting through the small doorway at the top, and stood there for a moment, catching his breath. The panorama before him was, quite simply, the best view in Edinburgh. The castle close behind him, the New Town spread out in front of him, sloping down towards the Firth of Forth*, with Fife*, Rebus's birthplace, visible in the distance. Calton Hill* … Leith* … Arthur's Seat* … and round to the castle
atemberaubend	again. It was breathtaking, or would have been had the breath not already been taken from him by the climb.
Brüstung	The parapet upon which he stood was incredibly narrow; again, there was hardly room enough to squeeze
überfüllt	past someone. How crowded did it get in the summer? Dangerously crowded? It seemed dangerously crowded just now, with only four people up here. He looked
Rand • steil abfallende Wand	over the edge upon the sheer drop to the gardens below, where a massing of tourists, growing restless at

info

Der größte Fluss Schottlands, der Forth, mündet bei Edinburgh in die Nordsee. Der so entstandene Meeresarm heißt Firth of Forth. Nördlich davon erstreckt sich die Grafschaft Fife. Edinburgh liegt am südlichen Ufer des Firth of Forth. Inspector Rebus lässt den Blick über die Stadt schweifen: über die georgianische New Town, die ab 1766 planmäßig angelegte Neustadt, den Hügel Calton Hill im Stadtzentrum, den Hafen Leith und den 231m hohen Hausberg Edinburghs. Der Arthur's Seat weist eine Vegetation auf, die man sonst nur in den schottischen Highlands findet. King Arthur soll von dort aus den Sieg seiner Armee über die Pikten beobachtet haben. Rebus' Rundblick endet beim Edinburgh Castle, dem ehemaligen Sitz der schottischen Könige.

being barred from the monument, stared up at him. Rebus shivered.

Not that it was cold. It was early June. Spring was finally late-blooming into summer, but that cold wind never left the city, that wind which never seemed to be warmed by the sun. It bit into Rebus now, reminding him that he lived in a northern climate. He looked down and saw Sir Walter's slumped body, reminding him why he was here.

'I thought we were going to have another corpse on our hands there for a minute.' The speaker was Detective Sergeant Brian Holmes. He had been in conversation with the police doctor, who himself was crouching over the corpse.

'Just getting my breath back,' Rebus explained.

'You should take up squash.'

'It's squashed enough up here.' The wind was nipping Rebus's ears. He began to wish he hadn't had that haircut at the weekend. 'What have we got?'

'Heart attack. The doctor reckons he was due for one anyway. A climb like that in an excited state. One of the witnesses says he just doubled over. Didn't cry out, didn't seem in pain ...'

weil ihnen der Zugang zum Monument verwehrt wurde • fröstelte • verwandelte sich ... wie ein Spätblüher in den Sommer • schnitt • und erinnerte • zusammengesunken • Leiche • in Hockstellung ... kauerte

mit ... anfangen • eng • kniff

glaubt • fällig • erregt • Zustand • Zeugen • brach ... zusammen

Übung 19

Ergänzen Sie die fehlenden Wörter aus den jeweiligen Wortfamilien, die auch im Text auf dieser Doppelseite zu finden sind:

noun	verb	adjective
breath		breathtaking
	to heighten	high
danger	to endanger	
speaker		English-speaking
scare	to scare	
excitement	to excite	

wehmütig	'Old mortality*, eh?' Rebus looked wistfully at the corpse. 'But why do you say he was excited?'
grinste • Plastiktüte • Notiz • Hülle	Holmes grinned. 'Think I'd bring you up here for the good of your health? Here.' He handed a polythene bag to Rebus. Inside the bag was a badly typed note. 'It was found in the binocular case.'
	Rebus read the note through its clear polythene window: GO TO TOP OF SCOTT MONUMENT. TUESDAY MIDDAY. I'LL BE THERE. LOOK FOR THE GUN.
stirnrunzelnd •	'The gun?' Rebus asked, frowning.
fuhr erschrocken hoch • Zeiger • Böllerschuss	There was a sudden explosion. Rebus started, but Holmes just looked at his watch, then corrected its hands. One o'clock. The noise had come from the blank charge fired every day from the castle walls at precisely one o'clock.
nur, dass • es würde ihm nichts ausmachen • richtete ... auf • spähten • winkte • senkte • begutachtete	'The gun,' Rebus repeated, except now it was a statement. Sir Walter's binoculars were lying beside him. Rebus lifted them – 'He wouldn't mind, would he?' – and fixed them on the castle. Tourists could be seen walking around. Some peered over the walls. A few fixed their own binoculars on Rebus. One, an elderly Asian, grinned and waved. Rebus lowered the binoculars. He examined them. 'These look brand new.'

info

Der Begriff old mortality heißt übersetzt „Alterssterblichkeit" und ist ein Hinweis auf das fortgeschrittene Alter des verstorbenen Kronanwalts Sir Walter Scott. Gleichzeitig spielt Inspector Rebus hier auf The Tale of Old Mortality, den Titel eines weiteren Romans von Sir Walter Scott, an.

'Bought for the purpose, I'd say, sir.'
'But what exactly *was* the purpose, Brian? What was he supposed to be looking at?' Rebus waited for an answer. None was forthcoming. 'Whatever it was,' Rebus went on, 'it as good as killed him. I suggest we take a look for ourselves.'
'Where, sir?'
Rebus nodded towards the castle. 'Over there, Brian. Come on.'
'Er, Inspector …?' Rebus looked towards the doctor, who was upright now, but pointing downwards with one finger. 'How are we going to get him down?'
Rebus stared at Sir Walter. Yes, he could see the problem. It would be hard graft taking him all the way back down the spiral stairs. What's more, damage to the body would be unavoidable. He supposed they could always use a winch and lower him straight to the ground … Well, it was a job for ambulancemen or undertakers, not the police. Rebus patted the doctor's shoulder.
'You're in charge, Doc,' he said, exiting through the door before the doctor could summon up a protest. Holmes shrugged apologetically, smiled, and followed

für diesen Zweck • sollte er
Sie blieb aus. • schlage vor
aufrecht stand • zeigte
Schinderei • Beschädigung • unvermeidbar • Winde • Sanitäter • Leichenbestatter • klopfte auf • verantwortlich • und verschwand • hervorbringen

Übung 20

Sind die folgenden Aussagen wahr oder falsch?
Tragen Sie ein T für true oder ein F für false in die Kästchen ein.

1. ☐ A gun that had been fired from the castle walls had killed Sir Walter Scott.
2. ☐ The binoculars round the dead man's neck were brand new.
3. ☐ He had received a note that had told him to climb to the top of the Scott Monument.
4. ☐ Sergeant Holmes had found the note in Sir Walter's pocket.
5. ☐ Inspector Rebus left the Sergeant in charge of getting the dead body down the spiral staircase.

Pfefferminzbonbon • steckte • herumkauen

Rebus into the dark. The doctor looked at the body, then over the edge, then back to the body again. He reached into his pocket for a mint, popped it into his mouth, and began to crunch on it. Then he, too, made for the door.

sinnierte • ihm fiel nichts ein

hatte sich nicht die Mühe gemacht • Eindruck • (Festungs-)Wall • Übertreibung • unmittelbar

verweilten ... nicht länger • jedoch

Splendour was falling on the castle walls*. Wrong poet, Rebus mused, but right image. He tried to recall if he'd ever read any Scott, but drew a blank. He thought he might have picked up *Waverley** once. As a colleague at the time had said, 'Imagine calling a book after the station.' Rebus hadn't bothered to explain; and hadn't read the book either, or if he had it had left no impression … He stood now on the ramparts, looking across to the Gothic exaggeration of the Scott Monument. A cannon was almost immediately behind him. Anyone wanting to be seen from the top of the monument would probably have been standing right on this spot. People did not linger here though. They might wander along the walls, take a few photographs, or pose for a few, but they would not stand in the one spot for longer than a minute or two.

Which meant, of course, that if someone *had* been

info

Rebus zitiert aus dem 1850 erschienenen Epos The Princess des Dichters Lord Tennyson. Die Originalzeile lautet: The splendour falls on castle walls. Rebus denkt bei der Betrachtung der Schlossmauern an „Glanz" und „Größe" (= splendour).
Waverley ist sowohl ein Buch von Sir Walter Scott als auch der Name des Edinburgher Bahnhofs (Waverley Station), der nach diesem Buch benannt wurde, nicht umgekehrt.
Viele Touristen besuchen das Denkmal, das einem Skye Terrier namens Bobby gesetzt wurde. Nach dem Tod seines Besitzers im Jahr 1858 verbrachte der Hund 14 Jahre – den Rest seines Lebens – am Grab seines Herrchens auf dem Friedhof neben der Greyfriars Kirk. Im nahe gelegenen Pub wurde Bobby täglich gefüttert.

standing here longer, they would be conspicuous. The problem was twofold: first, conspicuous to whom? Everyone else would be in motion, would not notice that someone was lingering. Second, all the potential witnesses would by now have gone their separate ways, in tour buses or on foot, down the Royal Mile or on to Princes Street, along George the Fourth Bridge to look at Greyfriars Bobby* …

auffällig • doppelt

The people milling around just now represented a fresh intake, new water flowing down the same old stream. Someone wanted to be seen by Sir Walter, and Sir Walter wanted to see him – hence the binoculars. No conversation was needed, just the sighting. Why? Rebus couldn't think of a single reason. He turned away from the wall and saw Holmes approaching. Meeting his eyes, Holmes shrugged his shoulders.
'I've talked to the guards on the gate. They don't remember seeing anyone suspicious. As one of them said, "All these bloody tourists look the same to me."'
Rebus smiled at this, but then someone was tugging at his sleeve, a small handbagged woman with sunglasses and thick lipstick.

die … umherliefen • Ladung

deshalb

näher kommen • zuckte mit den Schultern • verdächtig

zupfte • Ärmel

Übung 21

Ergänzen Sie die fehlenden Verbformen in den Bedingungssätzen. Beachten Sie dabei, dass im if-Satz kein will oder would stehen darf.
Beispiel:
Even if someone had lingered at the castle walls, nobody would have noticed.

1. If Sir Walter ______________________ (not, climb) up to the Monument, he wouldn't have died of a heart attack.
2. The guards might have noticed a suspicious person if there ______________________ (not, be) so many tourists.
3. If people hadn't given Bobby food, he ______________________ (not, survive).

'Sorry, could I ask you to move over a bit?' Her accent was American, her voice a nasal sing-song. 'Lawrence wants a picture of me with that gorgeous skyline behind me.' Rebus smiled at her, even made a slight bow, and moved a couple of yards out of the way, Holmes following suit.

'Thanks!' Lawrence called from behind his camera, freeing a hand so that he could wave it towards them. Rebus noticed that the man wore a yellow sticker on his chest. He looked back to the woman, now posing like the film star she so clearly wasn't, and saw that she too had a badge, her name – Diana – felt-tipped beneath some package company's logo.

'I wonder …' Rebus said quietly.

'Sir?'

'Maybe you were asking the wrong question at the gate, Brian. Yes, the right idea but the wrong question. Come on, let's go back and ask again. We'll see how eagle-eyed our friends really are.' They passed the photographer – his badge called him Larry rather than Lawrence – just as the shutter clicked.

'Great,' he said to nobody in particular. 'Just one more, sweetheart.' As he wound the film, Rebus paused and

hinreißend
Verbeugung • folgte seinem Beispiel
trug • Brust
Plakette • Pauschalreiseveranstalter
aufmerksam
Verschluss
vorspulte

Übung 22 In allen gesuchten Wörtern steckt der Buchstabe „e". Finden Sie die englischen Begriffe mithilfe der Erklärungen und Hinweise.

1. a large bird of prey that is said to have very good eyes
2. the organ that pumps blood through your body
3. extremely beautiful
4. the front part of your body between your neck and your stomach
5. a small piece of metal, cloth or plastic with a picture or words on it
6. someone who takes pictures professionally
7. to look at something carefully
8. the way someone pronounces words, showing which country or part of a country he or she comes from

stood beside him, then made a square from the thumb and forefinger of both hands and peered through it towards the woman Diana, as though assessing the composition of the picture. Larry caught the gesture. 'You a professional?' he asked, his tone just short of awe. 'Only in a manner of speaking, Larry,' said Rebus, turning away again. Holmes was left standing there, staring at the photographer. He wondered whether to shrug and smile again, as he had done with the doctor. What the hell. He shrugged. He smiled. And he followed Rebus towards the gate.

Viereck • Daumen • Zeigefinger • als ob er … beurteilte • grenzte an Ehrfurcht

Rebus went alone to the home of Sir Walter Scott, just off the Corstorphine Road near the zoo. As he stepped out of his car, he could have sworn he detected a faint wafting of animal dung. There was another car in the driveway, one which, with a sinking heart, he recognised. As he walked up to the front door of the house, he saw that the curtains were closed in the upstairs windows, while downstairs, painted wooden shutters had been pulled across to block out the daylight.
The door was opened by Superintendent 'Farmer' Watson.

hätte … schwören können • schwach • Hauch • was seine Stimmung deutlich vermieste • erkannte • Fensterläden

1. e _ _ _ e

2. _ e _ _ _

3. _ _ _ _ e _ _ _

4. _ _ e _ _

5. _ _ _ _ e

6. _ _ _ _ _ _ _ _ _ _ e _

7. _ e e _

8. _ _ _ e _ _

'I thought that was your car, sir,' Rebus said as Watson ushered him into the hall. When he spoke, the superintendent's voice was a whispered growl.
'He's still up there, you know.'
'Who?'
'Sir Walter, of course!' Flecks of saliva burst from the corners of Watson's mouth. Rebus thought it judicious to show not even the mildest amusement.
'I left the doctor in charge.'
'Dr Jameson couldn't organise a brewery visit. What the hell did you think you were doing?'
'I had ... *have* an investigation on my hands, sir. I thought I could be more usefully employed than playing undertaker.'
'He's stiff now, you know,' Watson said, his anger having diminished. He didn't exactly know why it was that he could never stay angry with Rebus; there was something about the man. 'They don't think they can get him down the stairs. They've tried twice, but he got stuck both times.' Rebus pursed his lips, the only way he could prevent them spreading into a wide grin. Watson saw this and saw, too, that the situation was not without a trace of humour.

hineinführte • geflüstert • Brummen

Spritzer • Speichel • klug

kriegt nichts auf die Reihe (wörtl. könnte nicht mal einen Brauereibesuch organisieren) • Ermittlung • beschäftigt • Groll • abgeschwächt • presste ... aufeinander • verhindern • Spur

Übung 23 Welche der angegebenen Möglichkeiten ist die richtige? Kreuzen Sie sie an.

1. Rebus expected Superintendent Watson to be at the Scotts' house.
- ☐ A colleague had told him that his boss would be there.
- ☐ Rebus had called him and asked him to come to the house.
- ☐ He had seen Watson's car in the driveway.

2. The Superintendent wasn't very happy that Rebus had left Dr Jameson in charge of Sir Walter's dead body, because
- ☐ the doctor was an alcoholic.
- ☐ the doctor wasn't very good at organising things.
- ☐ the doctor was needed somewhere else.

'Is that why you're here, sir? Placating the widow?' — um ... zu besänftigen
'No, I'm here on a personal level. Sir Walter and Lady Scott were friends of mine. That is, Sir Walter was, and Lady Scott still is.'
Rebus nodded slowly. Christ, he was thinking, the poor bugger's (Kerl) only been dead a couple of hours and here's old Farmer Watson already trying to ... But no, surely not. Watson was many things, but not callous (kaltschnäuzig •), not like that. Rebus rebuked (rügte) himself silently, and in so doing missed most of what Watson was saying.
' – in here.'
And a door from the hallway was being opened. Rebus was being shown into a spacious (geräumig) living-room – or were they called drawing-rooms in houses like this? Walking across to where Lady Scott sat by the fireside was like walking across a dance hall.
'This is Inspector Rebus,' Watson was saying. 'One of my men.'
Lady Scott looked up from her handkerchief (Taschentuch •). 'How do you do?' She offered him a delicate (zierlich •) hand, which he lightly touched with his own, in place of his usual firm (fest •) handshake. Lady Scott was in her mid fifties, a well-preserved (gut erhalten •) monument of neat (gepflegt) lines and precise move-

3. It was extremely difficult to move the dead body down the stairs because
- ☐ they couldn't find anyone who would do the job.
- ☐ there were too many tourists around blocking the stairs.
- ☐ the body was already stiff and got stuck in the spiral staircase.

4. The Scotts' living room was so big that it reminded Inspector Rebus of
- ☐ a dance hall.
- ☐ a golf course.
- ☐ the reception hall of a hotel.

ments. Rebus had seen her accompanying her husband to various functions in the city, had come across her photograph in the paper when he had received his knighthood. He saw, too, from the corner of his eye, the way Watson looked at her, a mixture of pity and something more than pity, as though he wanted at the same time to pat her hand and hug her to him.

wie sie … begleitete • in den Adelsstand erhoben worden war • Mitleid • umarmen

Who would want Sir Walter dead? That was, in a sense, what he had come here to ask. Still the question itself was valid. Rebus could think of adversaries – those Scott had crossed in his professional life, those he had helped put behind bars, those, perhaps, who resented everything from his title to the bright blue socks that had become something of a trademark after he admitted on a radio show that he wore no other colour on his feet …

zulässig • Feinde

hinter Gitter zu bringen • ein Ressentiment hatten gegen • Markenzeichen

'Lady Scott, I'm sorry to intrude on you at a time like this. I know it's difficult, but there are a couple of questions …'

• Sie zu belästigen

'Please, ask your questions.' She gestured for him to sit on the sofa – the sofa on which Farmer Watson had already made himself comfortable. Rebus sat down awkwardly. This whole business was awkward. He

bequem • unbeholfen

Übung 24 Welche Satzteile passen zusammen?
Tragen Sie den entsprechenden Buchstaben in die Kästchen ein.

1. ☐ Inspector Rebus had met Lady Scott before
2. ☐ Quite a number of people had been put to prison by Sir Walter.
3. ☐ Sir Walter's socks had become something of a trademark.
4. ☐ If you don't want to take a risk in a game of chess,
5. ☐ Lady Scott was absolutely sure that her husband didn't own a pair of binoculars.
6. ☐ Lady Scott didn't know
7. ☐ The note in the binocular case was not the only one.

knew the chess player's motto: if in doubt, play a pawn. Or as the Scots themselves would say, ca' canny. But that had never been his style, and he couldn't change now. As ever, he decided to sacrifice his queen.

'We found a note in Sir Walter's binocular case.'

'He didn't own a pair of binoculars.' Her voice was firm.

'He probably bought them this morning. Did he say where he was going?'

'No, just out. I was upstairs. He called that he was "popping out for an hour or two", and that was all.'

'What note?' This from Watson. What note indeed. Rebus wondered why Lady Scott hadn't asked the same thing.

'A typed note, telling Sir Walter to be at the top of the Scott Monument at midday.' Rebus paused, his attention wholly on Sir Walter's widow. 'There have been others, haven't there? Other notes?'

She nodded slowly. 'Yes. I found them by accident. I wasn't prying, I'm not like that. I was in Walter's office – he always called it that, his "office", never his study – looking for something, an old newspaper I think. Yes, there was an article I wanted to reread, and I'd

Schach • Zweifel • Bauer • sei vorsichtig • opfern

kurz weggehen würde

gänzlich

durch Zufall • ich habe nicht herumgeschnüffelt • noch einmal lesen

a) So he must have bought them on the morning before he went to the Scott Monument.

b) Lady Scott had found some more in her husband's office.

c) when she had accompanied Sir Walter on several occasions.

d) where her husband was going on the day of his death.

e) One of them might have taken revenge and caused Sir Walter's death.

f) He had only worn bright blue ones.

g) it is safer not to sacrifice the queen, but to play a pawn.

verflixt — searched high and low for the blessed paper. I was looking in Walter's office, and I found some … letters.'

rümpfte — She wrinkled her nose. 'He'd kept them quiet from me. Well, I suppose he had his reasons. I never said anything to him about finding them.' She smiled ruefully. 'I used to think sometimes that the unsaid was what kept our marriage alive. That may seem cruel. Now he's gone, I wish we'd told one another more …'

tupfte • feucht • gewickelt • drehte dabei • Binde, mit der man eine Wunde abschnürt — She dabbed at a liquid eye with the corner of her handkerchief, wrapped as it was around one finger, her free hand twisting and twisting the corners. To Rebus, it looked as if she were using it as a tourniquet.

'Do you know where these other notes are?' he asked.

'I don't know. Walter may have moved them.'

'Shall we see?'

unordentlich • verfügbar • Fläche • Stapel • vollgestopft • braune Umschläge • bestanden … aus • kunstvoll • abblätternd • Decke — The office was untidy in the best legal tradition: any available flat surface, including the carpet, seemed to be fair game for stacks of brown folders tied with ribbon, huge bulging manilla envelopes, magazines and newspapers, books and learned journals. Two walls consisted entirely of bookcases, from floor to near the ornate but flaking ceiling. One bookcase, glass-fronted, contained what Rebus reckoned must be the col-

Übung 25

Nur eine der angegebenen Antworten stimmt jeweils. Kreuzen Sie sie an.

1. Which of the following things could not be found in Sir Walter's office?

- ☐ a carpet
- ☐ a typewriter
- ☐ bookcases
- ☐ stacks of folders

2. Where had Sir Walter kept the letters that he had received?

- ☐ in a drawer of his desk
- ☐ under the carpet
- ☐ in a folder
- ☐ behind several books in the bookcase

lected works of the other Sir Walter Scott. The glass doors looked as though they hadn't been opened in a decade; the books themselves might never have been read. Still, it was a nice touch – to have one's study so thoroughly infiltrated by one's namesake.

'Ah, they're still here.' Lady Scott had slid a concertina-style folder out from beneath a pile of similar such files. 'Shall we take them back through to the morning-room?' She looked around her. 'I don't like it in here ... not now.'

Her Edinburgh accent, with its drawn vowels, had turned 'morning' into 'mourning'. Either that, thought Rebus, or she'd said 'mourning-room' in the first place. He would have liked to have stayed a little longer in Sir Walter's office, but was compelled to follow.

Jahrzehnt
vollständig • Ziehharmonika
langgezogen • Vokale • Trauer

Back in her chair, Lady Scott untied the ribbon around the file and let it fall open. The file itself was made up of a dozen or more compartments, but only one seemed to contain any paperwork. She pulled out the letters and handed them to Watson, who glanced through them wordlessly before handing them to Rebus.

knotete ... auf
Fächer
flüchtig durchsah

3. How did Lady Scott find the notes?
- She was cleaning the office.
- She was suspicious because of Sir Walter's strange behaviour.
- She was looking for a particular newspaper.
- She wanted to read a novel and found the notes in the bookcase.

4. What did Lady Scott not do after she had found the notes?
- She read the notes.
- She asked her husband what they meant.
- She put them back where she had found them.
- She never spoke to her husband about the notes.

Sir Walter had taken each note from its envelope, but had paper-clipped the envelopes to the backs of their respective notes. So Rebus was able to ascertain that the notes had been posted between three weeks and one week ago, and all bore a central London postmark. He read the three notes slowly to himself, then reread them. The first came quickly to its point.

mit einer Büroklammer ... befestigt • festzustellen • trugen

I ENCLOSE A LETTER. THERE ARE PLENTY MORE WHERE IT CAME FROM. YOU WILL HEAR FROM ME AGAIN.

lege ... bei

The second fleshed out the blackmail.

I HAVE ELEVEN MORE LETTERS. IF YOU'D LIKE THEM BACK, THEY WILL COST £2,000. GET THE MONEY.

machte ... deutlich • Erpressung

The third, posted a week ago, finalised things.

PUT THE MONEY IN A CARRIER BAG. GO TO THE CAFE ROYAL AT 9 P.M. FRIDAY. STAND AT THE BAR AND HAVE A DRINK. LEAVE THE BAG THERE AND GO MAKE A PHONE CALL. SPEND TWO MINUTES AWAY FROM THE BAR. WHEN YOU COME BACK, THE LETTERS WILL BE THERE.

legte ... endgültig fest • Tragetüte

Rebus looked up at Lady Scott. 'Did he pay?'

'I've really no idea.' 'But you could check?'

Übung 26 Vervollständigen Sie die Sätze, indem Sie die Verbformen in die Vergangenheit (simple past) setzen.

1. Sir Walter ________________ (hear) from the blackmailer again.
2. In his second note he ________________ (tell) Sir Walter that he ________________ (want) him to pay £ 2,000 for the embarrassing letters.
3. Sir Walter ________________ (get) the money from the bank and ________________ (put) it into a carrier bag.

'If you like, yes.'

Rebus nodded. 'I'd like to be sure.' The first note said that a letter was enclosed, obviously a letter concerning Sir Walter – but what kind of letter? Of the letter itself there was no sign. Twelve apparently incriminating or embarrassing letters for £2,000. A small price to pay for someone of Sir Walter's position in society. What's more, it seemed to Rebus a small price to *ask*. And if the exchange had taken place as arranged, what was the point of the last note, the one found in Sir Walter's binocular case? Yes, that was a point.

'Did you see the mail this morning, Lady Scott?'

'I was first to the door, yes.'

'And was there an envelope like these others?'

'I'm sure there wasn't.'

Rebus nodded. 'Yes, if there had been, I think Sir Walter would have kept it, judging by these.' He shook the notes – all with envelopes attached.

'Meaning, John?' Superintendent Watson sounded puzzled. To Rebus's ears, it was his natural voice.

'Meaning,' he explained, 'that the last note, the one we found on Sir Walter, was as it arrived at the house. No envelope. It must have been pushed through the letter-

concerning: betreffend
apparently: offenbar • incriminating: belastend • embarrassing: peinlich
point: Sinn
judging by: nach … zu urteilen • attached: angeheftet
puzzled: verwirrt

4. Then he ______________ (go) to the Café Royal, ______________ (have) a drink at the bar and ______________ (leave) the bag there.

5. When he ______________ (come) back a few minutes later, the money ______________ (be) gone, but he ______________ (find) the letters in the same place.

6. He ______________ (not, see) the blackmailer, though.

7. At home he ______________ (look) at the letters and ______________ (hide) them in his office.

8. But Sir Walter ______________ (not, say) anything about the letters to his wife.

box. I'd say sometime yesterday or this morning. The blackmail started in London, but the blackmailer came up here for the payoff. And he or she is still here – or was until midday. Now, I'm not so certain. If Sir Walter paid the money' – he nodded towards Lady Scott – 'and I *would* like you to check on that, please, today if possible. *If*, as I say, Sir Walter paid, *if* he got the letters back, then what was this morning's little game all about?'

Übergabe (des Erpressungsgeldes)

Watson nodded, arms folded, looking down into his lap as though seeking answers. Rebus doubted they'd be found so close to home. He rose to his feet.

verschränkt • Schoß • er … suchen würde • zweifelte daran • es wäre gut, wenn wir … fänden

'We could do with finding those letters, too. Perhaps, Lady Scott, you might have another look in your husband's … office.'

She nodded slowly. 'I should tell you, Inspector, that I'm not sure I *want* to find them.'

'I can understand that. But it would help us track down the blackmailer.'

ausfindig zu machen • gedämpft

Her voice was as low as the light in the room. 'Yes, of course.'

'And in the meantime, John?' Watson tried to sound like a man in charge of something. But there was a pleading edge to his voice.

flehend • Klang

Übung 27

Lösen Sie das Kreuzworträtsel mithilfe der folgenden Erklärungen:

Across →

1 to be uncertain about something
4 to call someone's name out in a public place
6 to look for something
7 The person who is responsible for a group or an activitiy is … .

Down ↓

2 opposite of loud or high
3 a list of the places you will visit on a journey
5 If someone says "yes" or nods, he or she gives her … .

'Meantime,' said Rebus, 'I'll be at the Castellain Hotel. The number will be in the book. You can always have me paged.' Watson gave Rebus one of his dark looks, the kind that said: I don't know what you're up to, but I can't let anyone else know that I *don't* know. Then he nodded and almost smiled.

mich ... ausrufen lassen

'Of course,' he said. 'Yes, off you go. I may stay on a little longer ...' He looked to Lady Scott for her assent. But she was busy with the handkerchief again, twisting and twisting and twisting ...

Zustimmung

The Castellain Hotel, a minute's walk from Princes Street, was a chaos of tourists. The large pot-planted lobby looked as though it was on someone's tour itinerary, with one large organised party about to leave, milling about as their luggage was taken out to the waiting bus by hard-pressed porters. At the same time, another party was arriving, the holiday company's representative conspicuous by being the only person who looked like he knew what was going on.

voller Kübelpflanzen • Reiseroute • im Begriff • gestresst

Seeing that a group was about to leave, Rebus panicked. But their lapel badges assured him that they were part of the Seascape Tours package. He walked up

Revers • versicherten

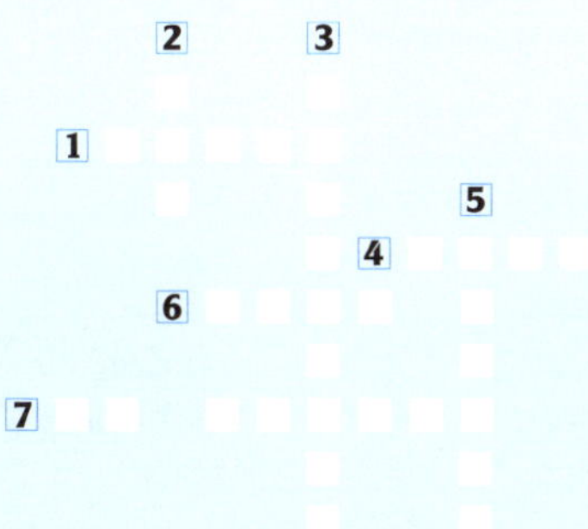

gestresst • Zweiteiler • Geschick • Gedränge • erklärte • Vertreterin • Hörer • wobei er … auswich • spannend

to the reception desk and waited while a harassed young woman in a tartan two-piece tried to take two telephone calls at the same time. She showed no little skill in the operation, and all the time she was talking her eyes were on the scrum of guests in front of her. Finally, she found a moment and a welcoming smile for him. Funny how at this time of year there were so many smiles to be found in Edinburgh …

'Yes, sir?'

'Detective Inspector Rebus,' he announced. 'I'd like a word with the Grebe Tours rep if she's around.'

'She's a he,' the receptionist explained. 'I think he might be in his room, hold on and I'll check.' She had picked up the telephone. 'Nothing wrong, is there?'

'No, nothing, just want a word, that's all.'

Her call was answered quickly. 'Hello, Tony? There's a gentleman in reception to see you.' Pause. 'Fine, I'll tell him. Bye.' She put down the receiver. 'He'll be down in a minute.'

Rebus nodded his thanks and, as she answered another telephone call, moved back into the reception hall, dodging the bags and the worried owners of the bags. There was something thrilling about holidaymakers.

Übung 28

Welche Wörter gehören zusammen?
Verbinden Sie sie mit einer Linie.

herd	desk
welcoming	holiday
pick up	gas
package	smile
reception	mentality
deserted	the telephone
laughing	beach

They were like children at a party. But at the same time there was something depressing, too, about the herd mentality. Rebus had never been on a package holiday in his life. He mistrusted the production-line cheerfulness of the reps and the guides. A walk along a deserted beach: now *that* was a holiday. Finding a pleasant out-of-the-way pub ... playing pinball so ruthlessly that the machine 'tilted' ... wasn't he due for a holiday himself? Not that he would take one: the loneliness could be a cage as well as a release. But he would never, he hoped, be as caged as these people around him. He looked for a Grebe Tours badge on any passing lapel or chest, but saw none. The Edinburgh Castle gatekeepers had been eagle-eyed all right, or one of them had. He'd recalled not only that a Grebe Tours bus had pulled in to the car park at around half past eleven that morning, but also that the rep had mentioned where the tour party was staying – the Castellain Hotel.

A small, balding man came out of the lift and fairly trotted to the reception desk, then, when the receptionist pointed towards Rebus, trotted over towards him, too. Did these reps take pills? potions? laughing gas? How the hell did they manage to keep it up?

bedrückend • Herdentrieb • Pauschal- • Fließband • Reiseführer • menschenleer • Flipper • schonungslos • kippte • Käfig • Befreiung

Wachen

mit schütter werdendem Haar • trottete • Zaubertränke

Übung 29

Mit der Verlaufsform in der Vergangenheit (past progressive) bringt man zum Ausdruck, dass eine Handlung länger andauerte. Ergänzen Sie die fehlenden Verbformen:

1. When Inspector Rebus arrived at the Castellain Hotel, the receptionist ____________________ (talk) to someone on the phone.

2. While Rebus ____________________ (wait) for the Grebe Tours representative, he ____________________ (watch) the tourists in the reception hall.

3. Rebus ____________________ (daydream) when he suddenly heard a man's voice saying "Hello!".

zu Ihren Diensten • zunehmend • Bauch • atemlos • ließ nach • Straßenräuber • Taschendieb • verletzt • hob • versicherte • Schützlinge • über • Schriftzug • Lust auf • Kriegsgebiet • während er vorausging • ziemlich

'Tony Bell at your service,' the small man said. They shook hands. Rebus noticed that Tony Bell was growing old. He had a swelling paunch and was a little breathless after his jog. He ran a hand over his baby-like head and kept grinning.

'Detective Inspector Rebus.' The grin subsided. In fact, most of Tony Bell's face seemed to subside.

'Oh Jesus,' he said, 'what is it? A mugger, pickpocket, what? Is somebody hurt? Which hospital?'

Rebus raised a hand. 'No need to panic,' he reassured him. 'Your charges are all quite safe.'

'Thank Christ for that.' The grin returned. Bell nodded towards a door, above which was printed the legend Dining-Room and Bar. 'Fancy a drink?'

'Anything to get out of this war zone,' Rebus said.

'You should see the bar after dinner,' said Tony Bell, leading the way, 'now *that's* a war zone …'

As Bell explained, the Grebe Tours party had a free afternoon. He checked his watch and told Rebus that they would probably start returning to the hotel fairly soon. There was a meeting arranged for before dinner, when the next day's itinerary would be discussed. Rebus told the rep what he wanted, and Bell himself

Übung 30 Sind die folgenden Aussagen wahr oder falsch?
Tragen Sie ein T für true oder ein F für false in die Kästchen ein.

1. ☐ Tony Bell, the Grebe Tours representative, was a small man with a bit of a belly.
2. ☐ When Tony Bell heard that Rebus was a police inspector, he was rather worried.
3. ☐ A member of the Grebe Tours party had been taken to hospital.
4. ☐ The two men continued their conversation at the hotel bar.
5. ☐ There were people from America, Canada and Australia in the Grebe Tours party.

suggested he stay put for the meeting. Yes, Rebus agreed, that seemed sensible, and meantime would Tony like another drink?
This particular Grebe Tours party was American. They'd flown in almost a month ago for what Bell called the 'Full British Tour' – Canterbury, Salisbury, Stonehenge, London, Stratford, York, the Lake District, Trossachs, Highlands, and Edinburgh.
'This is just about the last stop,' he said. 'For which relief much thanks, I can tell you. They're nice people, mind, I'm not saying they're not, but … demanding. Yes, that's what it is. If a Brit doesn't quite understand what's been said to him, or if something isn't *quite* right, or whatever, they tend to keep their gobs shut. But Americans …' He rolled his eyeballs. 'Americans,' he repeated, as though it explained all.
It did. Less than an hour later, Rebus was addressing a packed, seated crowd of forty American tourists in a room off the large dining-room. He had barely given them his rank when a hand shot into the air.
'Er … yes?'
The elderly woman stood up. 'Sir, are you from Scotland Yard?'

er solle an Ort und Stelle bleiben • vernünftig • speziell • Gruppe

worüber ich sehr erleichtert bin • wissen Sie • anstrengend

neigen dazu • Schnauzen

sprach zu

neben • kaum • Dienstrang

älter

6. The group had visited Italy and France before they came to Britain.

7. While Rebus was talking to Tony Bell, the party were on their way back from a trip to the Highlands.

8. There was a meeting before dinner, when the members of the group were informed about the next day's programme.

9. Rebus decided to stay for the meeting, because he wanted to ask a few questions.

10. An elderly lady told him that she knew an inspector from Scotland Yard.

11. A pickpocket is someone who breaks into houses and steals things.

Rebus shook his head. 'Scotland Yard's in London.' She was still standing. 'Now why is that?' she asked. Rebus had no answer to this, but someone else suggested that it was because that part of London was called Scotland Yard. Yes, but why was it called Scotland Yard in the first place? The woman had sat down now, but all around her was discussion and conjecture. Rebus looked towards Tony Bell, who rose from his own seat and succeeded in quietening things down. Eventually, Rebus was able to make his point. 'We're interested', he said, 'in a visitor to Edinburgh Castle this morning. You may have seen someone while you were there, someone standing by the walls, looking towards the Scott Monument. He or she might have been standing there for some time. If that means something to anybody, I'd like you to tell me about it. At the same time, it's possible that those of you who took photographs of your visit may have by chance snapped the person we're looking for. If any of you have cameras, I'd like to see the photos you took this morning.'
He was in luck. Nobody remembered seeing anyone suspicious – they were too busy looking at the sights. But two photographers had used polaroids, and anoth-

überhaupt erst • Mutmaßen

es schaffte, für Ruhe zu sorgen • schließlich

in Richtung

zufällig • geknipst

zu beschäftigt damit • Sofortbildkameras

Übung 31 Acht englische Begriffe sind in diesem Buchstabendickicht versteckt. Sie sind waagerecht (von links nach rechts), senkrecht (von oben nach unten) oder diagonal (von links oben nach rechts unten) angeordnet.

Die deutschen Entsprechungen der Wörter lauten:

verschwommen	beschäftigt
Fotoapparat	Streichholz
sich verstecken	für Ruhe sorgen
zugeben	in Richtung

er had taken his film into a same-day processor at lunchtime and so had the glossy photographs with him. Rebus studied these while Tony Bell went over the next day's arrangements with the group. The polaroid photos were badly taken, often blurry, with people in the background reduced to matchstick men. But the same-day photos were excellent, sharply focused 35 mm jobs.

hatte … am gleichen Tag entwickeln lassen
verschwommen • Hintergrund • Streichholz • eingestellt

As the tour party left the room, en route for dinner, Tony Bell came over to where Rebus was sitting and asked the question he knew he himself would be asked more than once over dinner.

'Any joy?'

'Maybe,' Rebus admitted. 'These two people keep cropping up.' He spread five photographs out in front of him. In two, a middle-aged woman was caught in the background, staring out over the wall she was leaning on. Leaning on, or hiding behind? In another two, a man in his late twenties or early thirties stood in similar pose, but with a more upright stance. In one photo, they could both be seen half turning with smiles on their faces towards the camera.

auf dem Weg
Glück gehabt? • räumte … ein • tauchen immer wieder auf • auf die sie sich lehnte • hinter der sie sich versteckte • Haltung

j	e	c	b	r	q	v	a	l	n	i	s
u	t	m	a	t	c	h	s	t	i	c	k
d	f	a	w	x	b	u	e	k	f	g	h
s	k	z	b	l	u	r	r	y	t	p	c
h	r	b	l	m	d	g	s	a	t	h	a
i	w	z	u	v	o	p	q	s	o	r	m
d	c	f	k	s	h	x	t	p	w	a	e
e	b	d	i	r	y	q	v	n	a	b	r
z	o	h	t	m	u	c	g	k	r	x	a
t	q	u	i	e	t	e	n	o	d	p	f
s	r	u	b	c	n	a	w	i	s	n	r
k	e	v	a	d	m	i	t	b	u	s	g

schüttelte • gesucht • letzte Reihe • nehme das zurück • Gabe • harmlos • beschwert sich • wohlgemerkt • sammelte ... ein • echt • bemuttert • Foto • Beerdigung • Reisebüro • Preisnachlass • Buchungen

'No.' Tony Bell was shaking his head. 'They might look like wanted criminals, but they're in our party. I think Mrs Eglinton was sitting in the back row near the door, beside her husband. You probably didn't see her. But Shaw Berkely was in the second row, over to one side. I'm surprised you didn't see him. Actually, I take that back. He has this gift of being innocuous. Never asks questions or complains. Mind you, I think he's seen most of this before.'

'Oh?' Rebus was gathering the photos together.

'He told me he'd been to Britain before on holiday.'

'And there's nothing between him and – ?' Rebus was pointing to the photograph of the man and woman together.

'Him and Mrs Eglinton?' Bell seemed genuinely amused. 'I don't know – maybe. She certainly mothers him a bit.' Rebus was still studying the print. 'Is he the youngest person on the tour?'

'By about ten years. Sad story really. His mother died, and after the funeral he said he just had to get away. Went into the travel agent's and we were offering a reduction for late bookings.'

'His father's dead too, then?'

Übung 32 Vervollständigen Sie die folgenden Sätzen mit den passenden Präpositionen.
(back, from, in, through, on, about, after, to, for)

1. During the meeting Mrs Eglinton was sitting __________ the back row.
2. In a party of tourists there is always someone who complains __________ everything.
3. Inspector Rebus flipped __________ the photos which a member of the Grebe Tours party had taken.

'That's right. I got his life story one night late in the bar. On a tour, I get everyone's story sooner or later.' — früher oder später

Rebus flipped through the sheaf of photos a final time. Nothing new presented itself to him. 'And you were at the castle between about half past eleven and quarter to one?' — blätterte • Bündel

'Just as I told you.'

'Oh well.' Rebus sighed. 'I don't think – ' — seufzte

'Inspector?' It was the receptionist, her head peering around the door. 'There's a call for you.'

It was Superintendent Watson. He was concise, factual. 'Withdrew five hundred pounds from each of four accounts, all on the same day, and in plenty of time for the rendezvous at the Cafe Royal.' — knapp • sachlich • (er) hob ... ab • Konten

'So presumably he paid up.' — vermutlich • bezahlte

'But did he get the letters back?'

'Mmm. Has Lady Scott had a look for them?'

'Yes, we've been through the study – not thoroughly, there's too much stuff in there for that. But we've had a look.' That 'we' sounded comfortable, sounded as though Watson had already got his feet under the table. 'So what now, John?' — gründlich • Zeug

'I'm coming over, if you've no objection, sir. With — wenn Sie keine Einwände haben

4. Tony Bell told Rebus that the young man had been __________ holiday in Britain before.

5. His mother had died and __________ the funeral he decided to get away from all the sad memories.

6. He went into the travel agent's and booked a package tour __________ England and Scotland.

7. Sir Walter had withdrawn two thousand pounds __________ his bank accounts.

8. Inspector Rebus didn't know whether Sir Walter had got the letters __________.

9. Lady Scott had looked __________ them in her husband's office, but hadn't found them.

respect, I'd like a look at Sir Walter's office for myself...' He went in search of Tony Bell, just so he could say thanks and goodbye. But he wasn't in the musty conference room, and he wasn't in the dining-room. He was in the bar, standing with one foot on the bar rail as he shared a joke with the woman he had called Mrs Eglinton. Rebus did not interrupt, but he did wink at the phone-bound receptionist as he passed her, then pushed his way out of the Castellain Hotel's double doors just as the wheezing of a bus's air brakes signalled the arrival of yet more human cargo.

bei allem Respekt • auf die Suche nach • muffig • Fußleiste • erzählte • zwinkerte ... zu • Quietschen • Druckluftbremsen • Fracht

There was no overhead lighting in Sir Walter Scott's study, but there were numerous floor lamps, desk lamps, and angle-poises. Rebus switched on as many as worked. Most were antiquated, with wiring to match, but there was one newish anglepoise attached to the bookcase, pointing inwards towards the collection of Scott's writings. There was a comfortable chair beside this lamp, and an ashtray on the floor between chair and bookcase.

When Watson put his head around the door, Rebus was seated in this chair, elbows resting on his knees, and

zahlreich • veraltet • Kabel • Aschenbecher • Ellbogen • gestützt

Übung 33 Ordnen Sie die folgenden Begriffe den drei verschiedenen Wortfeldern zu.
(angle-poise, cargo, palm, shelves, brakes, elbow, knee, bus, ashtray, tyres, head, chair)

vehicles (= Fahrzeuge)	
________________	________________
________________	________________

chin resting between the cupped palms of both hands. 'Margaret – that is, Lady Scott – she wondered if you wanted anything.'

'I want those letters.'

'I think she meant something feasible – like tea or coffee.'

Rebus shook his head. 'Maybe later, sir.'

Watson nodded, made to retreat, then thought of something. 'They got him down in the end. Had to use a winch. Not very dignified, but what can you do? I just hope the papers don't print any pictures.'

'Why don't you have a word with the editors, just to be on the safe side?'

'I might just do that, John.' Watson nodded. 'Yes, I might just do that.'

Alone again, Rebus rose from his chair and opened the glass doors of the bookcase. The position of chair, ashtray and lamp was interesting. It was as though Sir Walter had been reading volumes from these shelves, from his namesake's collected works. Rebus ran a finger over the spines. A few he had heard of; the vast majority he had not. One was titled *Castle Dangerous*. He smiled grimly at that. Dangerous, all right; or in Sir

Kinn • hohl • Handflächen

Machbares

wollte sich gerade zurückziehen • würdevoll • Herausgeber

Bände • Regale

Buchrücken • überwältigend • düster

parts of the body	things in a room
______	______
______	______
______	______
______	______

tödlich • richtete … aus • weiter • verwischt • glitt • (1 Inch = 2,54 cm) • gleichmäßig • Platz • Widerstand • zog • und umklammerte

Anziehungskraft

durchzugehen • mit Füllfederhalter geschrieben • Tag des Jüngsten Gerichts • Bildersprache • Jahrhundert

Walter's case, quite lethal. He angled the light farther into the bookcase. The dust on a row of books had been disturbed. Rebus pushed with one finger against the spine of a volume, and the book slid a good two inches back until it rested against the solid wall behind the bookcase. Two uniform inches of space for the whole of this row. Rebus reached a hand down behind the row of books and ran it along the shelf. He met resistance, and drew the hand out again, now clutching a sheaf of papers. Sir Walter had probably thought it as good a hiding place as any – a poor testament to Scott the novelist's powers of attraction. Rebus sat down in the chair again, brought the anglepoise closer, and began to sift through what he'd found.

There were, indeed, twelve letters, ornately fountain-penned promises of love with honour, of passion until doomsday. As with all such youthful nonsense, there was a lot of poetry and classical imagery. Rebus imagined it was standard private boys' school* stuff, even today. But these letters had been written half a century ago, sent from one schoolboy to another a year younger than himself. The younger boy was Sir Walter, and from the correspondence it was clear that Sir Wal-

info

In Großbritannien schicken reiche Eltern, insbesondere Angehörige der Oberschicht, ihre Kinder in der Regel auf Privatschulen, die als Internate geführt werden und meist nicht in gemischten Klassen unterrichten, sondern reine Mädchen- oder Jungenschulen sind. Diese Schulen werden auch public schools genannt, sind aber keine kostenlosen staatlichen Bildungseinrichtungen, sondern erheben Schulgeld. Auch Sir Walter ging auf eine derartige Privatschule für Jungen.

Die Abkürzung MP bedeutet Member of Parliament und bezeichnet einen ins britische Unterhaus (House of Commons) gewählten Abgeordneten.

ter's feelings for the writer had been every bit as inflamed as those of the writer himself.
Ah, the writer. Rebus tried to remember if he was still an MP*. He had the feeling he had either lost his seat, or else had retired. Maybe he was still on the go; Rebus paid little attention to politics. His attitude had always been: don't vote, it only encourages them. So, here was the presumed scandal. Hardly a scandal, but just about enough to cause embarrassment. At worst a humiliation. But then Rebus was beginning to suspect that humiliation, not financial profit, was the price exacted here.
And not even necessarily public humiliation, merely the private knowledge that someone knew of these letters, that someone had possessed them. Then the final taunt, the taunt Sir Walter could not resist: come to the Scott Monument, look across to the castle, and you will see who has been tormenting you these past weeks. You will know.
But now that same taunt was working on Rebus. He knew so much, yet in effect he knew nothing at all. He now possessed the 'what', but not the 'who'. And what should he do with the old love letters? Lady Scott had

entbrannt

war in Ruhestand gegangen • aktiv • Einstellung • wähle nicht • bestärkt • vermutet • Peinlichkeit • Demütigung • vermuten • der ... erzwungen wurde • öffentlich • lediglich • hatte ... besessen • Schmähung • widerstehen • gequält hat

doch

Übung 34

Ergänzen Sie in den folgenden Sätzen das jeweils passende Wort. (embarrassment, space, retired, fountain pen)

1. Behind the row of books in the shelf there was enough ____________________ to hide the sheaf of letters.

2. The letters had been written with a ____________________.

3. If someone had read the letters, this would have caused some ____________________ for Sir Walter.

4. Inspector Rebus didn't know whether the MP was still active in politics or whether he had already ____________________.

vernichten • aushändigen • ungelesen • entdecken • Geheimnis • mehrdeutig • beunruhigen • erzielt hast • streichelst • Rugbytraining • zurücklegen • sich ihrer annehmen • strich • fest • festgeklemmt • löste … ab • befestigt • Promenade • nachdenklich • umwickeln

said she wasn't sure she wanted to find them. He could take them away with him – destroy them. Or he could hand them over to her, tell her what they were. It would be up to her either to destroy them unread or to discover this silly secret. He could always say: It's all right, it's nothing really … Mind you, some of the sentences were ambiguous enough to disturb, weren't they? Rebus read again. 'When you scored 50 n.o.* and afterwards we showered …' 'When you stroke me like that …' 'After rugger practice …'

Ach. He got up and opened the bookcase again. He would replace them. Let time deal with them; he could not. But in placing his hand back down behind the line of books, he brushed against something else, not paper but stiff card. He hadn't noticed it before because it seemed stuck to the wall. He peeled it carefully away and brought it into the light. It was a photograph, black and white, ten inches by eight and mounted on card. A man and woman on an esplanade, arm in arm, posing for the photographer. The man looked a little pensive, trying to smile but not sure he actually wanted to be caught like this. The woman seemed to wrap both her arms round one of his,

info

Diese Abkürzung wird beim Cricket verwendet, einem Ballspiel, bei dem sich zwei Mannschaften mit jeweils elf Spielern abwechselnd als Schlagmannschaft und Feldmannschaft gegenüberstehen. Bleibt der Schlagmann in einer Runde lange an der Reihe, ist er not out, das heißt „nicht ausgeschieden". Die Zahl vor der Abkürzung gibt Auskunft über die erreichten Punkte.

Mannschaftssportarten wie Cricket und Rugby galten als besonders geeignet, Teamgeist und Disziplin zu fördern und zur Charakterbildung beizutragen. Daher wurde und wird ihnen auch heute noch an den Privatschulen große Bedeutung beigemessen.

restraining him; and she was laughing, thrilled by this moment, thrilled to be with him.
The man was Sir Walter. A Sir Walter twenty years older than the schoolboy of the love letters, mid thirties perhaps. And the woman? Rebus stared long and hard at the woman. Put the photograph down and paced the study, touching things, peering through the shutters. He was thinking and not thinking. He had seen the woman before somewhere … but where? She was not Lady Scott, of that he was certain. But he'd seen her recently, seen that face … that face.
And then he knew. Oh yes, he knew.
He telephoned the Castellain, half listening as the story was given to him. Taken ill suddenly … poorly … decided to go home … airport … flying to London and catching a connection tonight … Was there a problem? Well, of course there was a problem, but no one at the hotel could help with it, not now. The blackmail over, Rebus himself had inadvertently caused the blackmailer to flee. He had gone to the hotel hoping – such a slim hope – for help, not realising that one of the Grebe Tours party was his quarry. Once again, he had sacrificed his queen too early in the game.

und hielt ihn fest • außer sich vor Freude

ging … auf und ab • berührte

vor Kurzem

erkrankt

Anschlussflug

unbeabsichtigterweise • fliehen • schwach • Beute

Übung 35

Bringen Sie die folgenden Sätze in die richtige chronologische Reihenfolge. Tragen Sie die Nummern in die Kästchen ein.

- [1] Inspector Rebus wasn't sure what to do with the letters.
- [ ] Reaching down behind the line of books, he brushed against a stiff card.
- [ ] Rebus looked at the woman's face and suddenly realized where he had seen a face like hers before.
- [ ] He decided to put them back where he had found them.
- [ ] When he got it out, he saw that it was a photograph.
- [ ] It showed a man – Sir Walter in his thirties – and a woman with her arms wrapped around his.

He telephoned Edinburgh Airport, only to be told that the flight had already taken off. He asked to be rerouted to Security, and asked them for the name of the security chief at Heathrow. He was calling Heathrow when Watson appeared in the hall.

weiterverbunden zu werden

erschien

'Making quite a few calls, aren't you, John? Not personal, I hope.'

Rebus ignored his superior as his call was connected. 'Mr Masterson in Security, please,' he said. And then: 'Yes, it is urgent. I'll hold.' He turned to Watson at last. 'Oh, it's personal all right, sir. But it's nothing to do with me. I'll tell you all about it in a minute. Then we can decide what to tell Lady Scott. Actually, seeing as you're a friend of the family and all, *you* can tell her. That'd be best, wouldn't it, sir? There are some things only your friends can tell you, after all, aren't there?'

Vorgesetzter • da die Verbindung zustande kam • dringend

He was through to Heathrow Security, and turned away from Watson the better to talk with Masterson. The superintendent stood there, dimly aware that Rebus was going to force him to tell Margaret something she would probably rather not hear. He wondered if she would ever again have time for the person who would tell her … And he cursed John Rebus, who

vage • sich bewusst • lieber

verfluchte

Übung 36 Lösen Sie das Wörterrätsel mithilfe der Erklärungen.

1. giving strong loyal support
2. to say or think bad things about someone because you are angry
3. to start to be seen
4. your physical condition
5. very important and calling for immediate attention
6. to tell a story that is not true
7. to make something dirty
8. having realized something

was so good at digging yet never seemed to soil his own hands. It was a gift, a terrible, destructive gift. Watson, a staunch believer in the Christian God, doubted Rebus's gift had come down from on high. No, not from on high.

Herumwühlen • schmutzig zu machen • überzeugt

The phone call was ending. Rebus put down the receiver and nodded towards Sir Walter's study.

'If you'll step into the office, sir,' he said, 'there's something I'd like to show you …'

Shaw Berkely was arrested at Heathrow, and, despite protestations regarding his health and cries for consular aid, was escorted back to Edinburgh, where Rebus was waiting, brisk and definitive, in Interview Room A of Great London Road Police Station.

trotz • Protesterklärungen • Gesundheit • forsch

Berkely's mother had died two months before. She had never told him the truth about his birth, spinning instead some story about his father being dead. But in sorting through his mother's papers, Shaw discovered the truth – several truths, in fact.

und spann • stattdessen

His mother had been in love with Walter Scott, had become pregnant by him, but had been, as she herself

schwanger

Superintendent Watson is Inspector Rebus'

1. S
2. U
3. P
4. E
5. R
6. I
7. O
8. R

fallen gelassen • zu Gunsten von • floh • Enthüllung • zu Wohlstand gekommen war • Leid • Wut • auf … stieß

put it in her journal, 'discarded' in favour of the 'better marriage' provided by Margaret Winton-Addams. Shaw's mother accepted some money from Scott and fled to the United States, where she had a younger sister. Shaw grew up believing his father dead. The revelation not only that he was alive, but that he had prospered in society after having caused Shaw's mother misery and torment, led to a son's rage. But it was impotent rage, Shaw thought, until he came across the love letters. His mother must at some point have stolen them from Scott, or at least had come out of the relationship in possession of them. Shaw decided on a teasing revenge, knowing Scott would deduce that any blackmailer in possession of the letters was probably also well informed about his affair and the bastard son. He used the tour party as an elaborate cover (and also, he admitted, because it was a cheap travel option). He brought with him to Britain not only the letters, but also the series of typed notes. The irony was that he had been to Edinburgh before, had studied there for three months as part of some exchange with his American college. He knew now why his mother, though proud of the scholarship, had been against his going.

Beziehung • ihn aus Rache zu quälen • folgern

raffiniert • Tarnung

Austausch

Stipendium

Übung 37

Welche der angegebenen Möglichkeiten ist die richtige? Kreuzen Sie sie an.

1. Shaw Berkely, one of the Grebe Tours party, was
- ☐ Sir Walter's former schoolmate who had written the letters.
- ☐ Sir Walter's son.
- ☐ Sir Walter's nephew.

2. Shaw Berkely wanted to take revenge on Sir Walter because
- ☐ Sir Walter had promised but not given him a sum of money.
- ☐ Sir Walter had refused to see him when he had studied in Edinburgh for three months.
- ☐ Sir Walter had made his mother unhappy.

For three months he had lived in his father's city, yet hadn't known it.

He sent the notes from London – the travel party's base for much of its stay in England. The exchange – letters for cash – had gone ahead in the Cafe Royal, the bar having been a haunt of his student days. But he had known his final note, delivered by hand, would tempt Sir Walter, would lead him to the top of the Scott Monument. No, he said, he hadn't just wanted Sir Walter to see him, to see the son he had never known. Shaw had much of the money on him, stuffed into a money belt around his waist. The intention had been to release wads of money, Sir Walter's money, down on to Princes Street Gardens.

'I didn't mean for him to die … I just wanted him to know how I felt about him … I don't know. But Jesus' – he grinned – 'I still wish I'd let fly with all that loot.'

Rebus shuddered to think of the ramifications. Stampede in Princes Street! Hundreds dead in lunchtime spree! Biggest *scoor-oot** ever! No, best not to think about it. Instead, he made for the Cafe Royal himself. It was late morning, the day after Berkely's arrest. The pub was quiet as yet, but Rebus was surprised to see Dr

Standort • Aufenthalt • Bargeld • Stammlokal • abgeliefert • in Versuchung führen

hineingestopft • Gürteltasche • Taille • Bündel

Knete • schauderte • Auswirkungen • Massenpanik • Amoklauf

3. The notes that Berkely sent to Sir Walter's house had been typed

- before he set off to Britain.
- in a hotel in London.
- in the Café Royal.

info

Bei einer schottischen Hochzeit wirft die Braut Münzen, die die Kinder aufsammeln und natürlich behalten dürfen. Diesen Brauch nennt man scoor-oot. Er soll auf die Hochzeit von Queen Mary und ihrem zweiten Mann, Lord Darnley, zurückgehen. Queen Mary hatte damals Mitleid mit den armen Leuten, die vor den Toren von Holyrood Palace standen, um das Brautpaar zu sehen. Daher ordnete sie an, dass Geld für sie über das Tor geworfen werden soll.

Jameson standing at the bar, fortifying himself with what looked suspiciously like a double whisky. Remembering how he had left the doctor in the lurch regarding Sir Walter's body, Rebus grinned broadly and offered a healthy slap on the back.

'Morning, Doc, fancy seeing you in here.' Rebus leaned his elbows on the bar. 'We mustn't be keeping you busy enough.' He paused. There was a twinkle in his eye as he spoke. 'Here, let me get you a stiff one …' And he laughed so hard even the waiters from the Oyster Bar came to investigate. But all they saw was a tall, well-built man leaning against a much smaller, more timid man, and saying as he raised his glass: 'Here's to mortality, to old mortality!'

So all in all it was just another day in the Cafe Royal.

und stärkte sich • hängen gelassen hatte • breit • ordentlich • Klaps • so was, Sie hier zu sehen • Funkeln • um nachzusehen • hob • auf die

Übung 38

Der Autor Ian Rankin verwendet in der Geschichte eine Reihe von umgangssprachlichen Ausdrücken. Inspector Rebus hatte den Doktor „hängen lassen“, hatte aber nicht unbedingt ein schlechtes Gewissen deswegen.

Der Doktor saß also in der „Klemme“. Im Englischen gibt es dafür drei verschiedene Ausdrücke. Welche sind die richtigen? Kreuzen Sie an.

The doctor was in a

☐ jam.	☐ mess.	☐ fix.
☐ tight spot.	☐ gap.	☐ set.

Facing the Music

AN INSPECTOR REBUS STORY

Dafür geradestehen (Wortspiel)

An unmarked police car.
Interesting phrase, that. Inspector John Rebus's car, punch-drunk and weather-beaten, scarred and mauled, would still merit description as 'unmarked', despite the copious evidence to the contrary. Oily-handed mechanics stifled grins whenever he waddled into a forecourt. Garage proprietors adjusted the thick gold rings on their fingers and reached for the calculator.
Still, there were times when the old war-horse came in handy. It might or might not be 'unmarked'; unremarkable it certainly was. Even the most cynical law-breaker would hardly expect CID* to spend their time sitting around in a breaker's-yard special. Rebus's car was a must for undercover work, the only problem coming if the villains decided to make a run for

nicht gekennzeichnet • verbeult • verschrammt • beschädigt • reichlich • unterdrückten • Vorplatz • Besitzer • Taschenrechner • praktisch war • wenig bemerkenswert • Schrottauto

Schurken

info

Im Verlauf der Geschichte verwendet der Autor Ian Rankin mehrere Abkürzungen, die sich auf den Polizeidienst beziehen.

CID ist die Kurzform für Criminal Investigation Department, auf Deutsch: Kripo.

Die Personen, die in der Geschichte vorkommen, haben folgende Dienstgrade (in der Polizeihierarchie von oben nach unten):

Chief Super(intendent):	Kriminalhauptkommissar
Detective Inspector (DI):	Kriminalkommissar
Detective Sergeant (DS):	Kriminalhauptmann
Detective Constable (DC):	Kriminalwachtmeister

schwach • es … abhängen • zu seiner Verteidigung • Körperform • Kontur, Form • Seufzer • wiederholte

it. Then, even the most elderly and infirm could outpace it.
'But it's a stayer,' Rebus would say in mitigation.
He sat now, the driving-seat so used to his shape that it formed a mould around him, stroking the steering-wheel with his hands. There was a loud sigh from the passenger seat, and Detective Sergeant Brian Holmes repeated his question.
'Why have we stopped?'

einige • bewölkt • Windböen • vermutlich • sich gegenseitig zu übertreffen • peitschte • betäubt • gefühllos • Teegebäck • Fußgänger • Mitleid • brötchenartiges Mürbgebäck

Rebus looked around him. They were parked by the side of Queensferry Street, only a couple of hundred yards from Princes Street's west end. It was early afternoon, overcast but dry. The gusts of wind blowing in from the Firth of Forth were probably keeping the rain away. The corner of Princes Street, where Fraser's department store and the Caledonian Hotel tried to outstare one another, caught the winds and whipped them against unsuspecting shoppers, who could be seen, dazed and numb, making their way afterwards along Queensferry Street, in search of coffee and shortcake. Rebus gave the pedestrians a look of pity. Holmes sighed again. He could murder a pot of tea and some fruit scones with butter.

Übung 39 Welche der angegebenen Antworten ist die richtige?

1. What was the car like that Inspector Rebus was driving?
- ☐ He was driving a black-and-white police car.
- ☐ It was rather old and shabby.
- ☐ His car didn't look new but it was a fast sports car.

2. Inspector Rebus said: "I've never been called to any sort of crime on this street." Which street is he referring to?
- ☐ Queensferry Street
- ☐ Princes Street
- ☐ Firth of Forth Street

'Do you know, Brian,' Rebus began, 'in all the years I've been in Edinburgh, I've never been called to any sort of a crime on this street.' He slapped the steering-wheel for emphasis. 'Not once.' 'Maybe they should put up a plaque,' suggested Holmes.
Rebus almost smiled. 'Maybe they should.'
'Is that why we're sitting here? You want to break your duck?' Holmes glanced into the tea-shop window, then away again quickly licking dry lips. 'It might take a while, you know,' he said.
'It might, Brian. But then again …'
Rebus tapped out a tattoo on the steering-wheel. Holmes was beginning to regret his own enthusiasm. Hadn't Rebus tried to deter him from coming out for this drive? Not that they'd driven much. But anything, Holmes reasoned, was better than catching up on paperwork. Well, just about anything.
'What's the longest time you've been on a stake-out?' he asked, making conversation.
'A week,' said Rebus. 'Protection racket run from a pub down near Powderhall. It was a joint operation with Trading Standards. We spent five days pretending to be on the broo, playing pool all day.'

schlug auf • Lenkrad • um dem Ganzen Nachdruck zu verleihen • Gedenktafel • diese Tradition brechen • warf einen Blick • trommelte mit den Fingern • zu bereuen • ihn davon abzuhalten • überlegte • abzuarbeiten • Observierung • Schutzgelderpressung • gemeinsam • Handelsaufsichtsbehörde • so zu tun als ob • arbeitslos

3. Why had Detective Sergeant Holmes come with Inspector Rebus?

- ☐ The Chief Superintendent had told him to accompany Inspector Rebus.
- ☐ Rebus had promised him to stop at a café for tea and scones.
- ☐ He didn't feel like doing paperwork in the office.

'Did you get a result?'
'We beat them at pool,' Rebus said.
There was a yell from a shop doorway, just as a young man was sprinting across the road in front of their car. The young man was carrying a black metal box. The person who'd called out did so again.
'Stop him! Thief! Stop him!'
The man in the shop doorway was waving, pointing towards the sprinter. Holmes looked towards Rebus, seemed about to say something, but decided against it. 'Come on then!' he said.
Rebus started the car's engine, signalled, and moved out into the traffic. Holmes was focusing through the windscreen. 'I can see him. Put your foot down!'
'"Put your foot down, *sir*",' Rebus said calmly. 'Don't worry, Brian.'
'Hell, he's turning into Randolph Place.'
Rebus signalled again, brought the car across the oncoming traffic, and turned into the dead end that was Randolph Place. Only, while it was a dead end for cars, there were pedestrian passages either side of West Register House. The young man, carrying the narrow box under his arm, turned into one of the passages.

schlugen • beim Pool-Billard • Schrei • Dieb • fuchtelte • zeigte in Richtung • schien im Begriff zu sein • Motor • blinkte • schaute konzentriert • Windschutzscheibe • Geben Sie Gas! • verdammt • Gegenverkehr • Sackgasse • auf beiden Seiten

Übung 40 In jeder Zeile steht ein Wort, das nicht zu den anderen passt. Streichen Sie es durch.

1. engine – windscreen – yell – steering wheel
2. dead end – fault – pedestrian passage – traffic lights
3. to leap – to sprint – to walk – to agree
4. narrow – calmly – carefully – loudly
5. to wave – to point – to step – to flap

Rebus pulled to a halt. Holmes had the car door open before it had stopped, and leapt out, ready to follow on foot.
'Cut him off!' he yelled, meaning for Rebus to drive back on to Queensferry Street, around Hope Street and into Charlotte Square, where the passage emerged.
'"Cut him off, *sir*",' mouthed Rebus.
He did a careful three-point turn, and just as carefully moved back out into traffic held to a crawl by traffic lights. By the time he reached Charlotte Square and the front of West Register House, Holmes was shrugging his shoulders and flapping his arms. Rebus pulled to a stop beside him.
'Did you see him?' Holmes asked, getting into the car.
'No.'
'Where have you been anyway?'
'A red light.'
Holmes looked at him as though he were mad. Since when had Inspector John Rebus stopped for a red light? 'Well, I've lost him anyway.'
'Not your fault, Brian.'
Holmes looked at him again. 'Right,' he agreed. 'So, back to the shop? What was it anyway?'

hielt den Wagen an • sprang hinaus • Schneiden Sie ihm den Weg ab! • schrie • herauskam • sagte ... überdeutlich • wendete ... in drei Zügen • der fast zum Stehen gebracht wurde • Ampel • wedelte mit den Armen

als ob

Schuld • stimmte ... zu

Übung 41

Ordnen Sie die folgenden Wörter den passenden Erklärungen zu:
(to pull to a halt, traffic, to turn, to agree, thief, to beat someone)

someone who steals things: ______________________

to get more points in a game or competition: ______________

to make something stop moving: ______________________

the vehicles moving along a street: ____________________

to have the same opinion about something: ______________

to change directions: ______________________________

'Hi-fi shop, I think.'
Holmes nodded as Rebus moved off again into the traffic. Yes, the box had the look of a piece of hi-fi, some slim rack component. They'd find out at the shop. But instead of doing a circuit of Charlotte Square to take them back into Queensferry Street, Rebus signalled along George Street. Holmes, still catching his breath, looked around disbelieving. 'Where are we going?'
'I thought you were fed up with Queensferry Street. We're going back to the station.'
'*What?*'
'Back to the station.'
'But what about – ?'
'Relax, Brian. You've got to learn not to fret so much.'
Holmes examined his superior's face. 'You're up to something,' he said at last.
Rebus turned and smiled. 'Took you long enough,' he said.

nickte • dünn • Teil einer Stereoanlage • um ... herumzufahren • ungläubig • Sie hätten die Nase voll von • Polizeirevier • sich nicht ... aufzuregen • seines Vorgesetzten • Sie führen etwas im Schilde

But whatever it was, Rebus wasn't telling. Back at the station, he went straight to the main desk.
'Any robberies, Alec?' The desk officer had a few. The most recent was a snatch at a specialist hi-fi shop.

geradewegs • Raubüberfälle • Raub

Übung 42 Die Sätze in dieser Übung stehen im Aktiv. Wandeln Sie sie in eine Passivkonstruktion (in derselben Zeitstufe) um.
Verwenden Sie den by-agent nur dann, wenn genauere Angaben vorliegen, von wem etwas getan wird bzw. wurde.

Beispiele:

Aktiv: Someone has stolen a CD player from a hi-fi shop.
Passiv: A CD player has been stolen from a hi-fi shop.

Aktiv: The shop owner reported the crime to the police.
Passiv: The crime was reported to the police by the shop owner.

'We'll take that,' said Rebus. The desk officer blinked. 'It's not much, sir. Just a single item, thief did a runner.' 'Nevertheless, Alec,' said Rebus. 'A crime has been committed, and it's our duty to investigate it.' He turned to head back out to the car.
'Is he all right?' Alec asked Holmes.
Holmes was beginning to wonder, but decided to go along for the ride anyway.

blinzelte • einzig • Gegenstand • floh zu Fuß • trotzdem • ist verübt worden • in dieser Sache zu ermitteln

'A cassette deck,' the proprietor explained. 'Nice model, too. Not top of the range, but nice. Top-of-the-range stuff isn't kept out on the shop floor. We keep it in the demonstration rooms.'
Holmes was looking at the shelf where the cassette deck had rested. There were other decks either side of the gap, more expensive decks at that.
'Why would he choose that one?' Holmes asked. 'Eh?'
'Well, it's not the dearest, is it? And it's not even the closest to the door.'
The dealer shrugged. 'Kids these days, who can tell?' His thick hair was still tousled from where he had stood in the Queensferry Street wind-tunnel, yelling against the elements as passers-by stared at him.

Spitzenmodell • Zeug • Laden

Regal

Lücke • teurer • aussuchen • das Teuerste

Händler • zuckte mit den Schultern • zerzaust • Passanten

1. The thief had knocked over a CD shelf.
A CD shelf ______________________________

2. Some passers-by gave Inspector Rebus a description of the thief.
A description of the thief ______________________________
____

3. Someone committed a murder last night.
A murder ______________________________

4. They have sent a specialist to the scene of the crime.
A specialist ______________________________

ich gehe davon aus • Versicherung • Lautsprecher • Punktesystem • Jungs • kümmert euch nicht darum • Formulare • verblüfft

'I take it you've got insurance, Mr Wardle?' The question came from Rebus, who was standing in front of a row of loudspeakers.

'Christ yes, and it costs enough.' Wardle shrugged. 'Look, it's okay. I know how it works. Points system, right? Anything under a four-point crime, and you lads don't bother. You just fill out the forms so I can claim from the insurance. What does this rate? One point? Two at the most?' Rebus blinked, perhaps stunned by the use of the word 'lads' in connection with him.

Beschreibung • in der Zwischenzeit • Bestand • gewöhnlich • Kette • sinnierte • ein Einbrecher, der ein Schaufenster mit dem Auto auframmt

'You've got the serial number, Mr Wardle,' he said at last. 'That'll give us a start. Then a description of the thief – that's more than we usually get in cases of shop-snatching. Meantime, you might move your stock a bit further back from the door and think about a common chain or circuit alarm so they can't be taken off their shelves. Okay?' Wardle nodded.

'And be thankful,' mused Rebus. 'After all, it could've been worse. It could have been a ram-raider.' He picked up a CD case from where it sat on top of a machine: Mantovani and his Orchestra. 'Or even a critic,' said Rebus.

Übung 43 Lösen Sie das Kreuzworträtsel mithilfe der Erklärungen:

Down ↓

1 to make someone extremely angry
2 covered with many small spots
3 an official document
4 a boy or young man

Across →

5 music comes out of them
6 joined rings that are used for keeping something locked or safe
7 easily set on fire

Back at the station, Holmes sat fuming like a readying volcano. Or at least like a tin of something flammable left for too long in the sun.

Whatever Rebus was up to, as per usual he wasn't saying. It infuriated Holmes. Now Rebus was off at a meeting in the Chief Super's office: nothing very important, just routine … like the snatch at the hi-fi shop.

Holmes played the scene through in his mind. The stationary car, causing an obstruction to the already slow movement of traffic. Then Wardle's cry, and the youth running across the road, jinking between cars. The youth had half turned, giving Holmes a moment's view of a cheek speckled with acne, cropped spiky hair. A skinny runt of a sixteen-year-old in faded jeans and trainers. Pale blue windcheater with a lumberjack shirt hanging loose below its hemline.

And carrying a hi-fi component that was neither the easiest piece in the shop to steal, nor the dearest. Wardle had seemed relaxed about the whole affair. The insurance would cover it. An insurance scam: was that it? Was Rebus working on some insurance diddle on the q.t., maybe as a favour to some investigator from the Pru? Holmes hated the way his superior worked,

und rauchte vor Wut • leicht entzündbar

machte wütend • Hauptkommissar • stehend • Behinderung • Jugendlicher • und sich … durchschlängelte • gesprenkelt • mit kurzem Igelhaarschnitt • Zwerg • Windjacke • Saum

Betrug • Schwindel • heimlich • Gefallen • (Versicherungsgesell.)

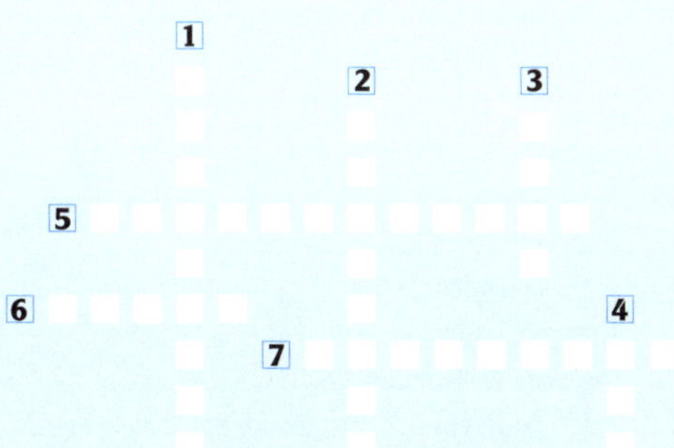

ballverliebt • der ... nicht abgab • Seitenlinie • sich ... weigerte • niedergemäht • Klugscheißer

like a greedy if talented footballer hogging the ball, dribbling past man after man, getting himself trapped beside the by-line but still refusing to pass the ball. Holmes had known a boy at school like that. One day, fed up, Holmes had scythed the smart-arse down, even though they'd been on the same side ...

hatte er einen Tipp bekommen • Es ergab keinen Sinn.

Rebus had known the theft would take place. Therefore, he'd been tipped off. Therefore, the thief had been set up. There was just one big *but* to the whole theory – Rebus had let the thief get away. It didn't make sense. It didn't make any sense at all. 'Right,' Holmes said, nodding to himself. 'Right you are, sir.' And with that, he went off to find the young offender files.

Straftäter • Akten

That evening, just after six, Rebus thought that since he was in the area anyway, he'd drop into Mr Wardle's home and report the lack of progress on the case. It might be that, time having passed, Wardle would remember something else about the snatch, some crucial detail. The description he'd been able to give of the thief had been next to useless. It was almost as though he didn't want the hassle, didn't want the thief caught. Well, maybe Rebus could jog his memory.

dass es keine Fortschritte gab • entscheidend

Theater • auf die Sprünge helfen

Übung 44

Sind die folgenden Aussagen wahr oder falsch?
Tragen Sie ein T für true oder ein F für false in die Kästchen ein.

1. ☐ Sergeant Holmes had been so angry with a boy in his football team that he had scythed him down.
2. ☐ Inspector Rebus told Holmes to check the young offender files.
3. ☐ Holmes spotted the young lad who had stolen the cassette deck in the files.
4. ☐ Inspector Rebus had arrested Jib Bankhead several times.
5. ☐ Rebus was extremely pleased that Sergeant Holmes had found the thief.

The radio came to life. It was a message from DS Holmes. And when Rebus heard it, he snarled and turned the car back around towards the city centre.

Funkgerät • knurrte

It was lucky for Holmes, so Rebus said, that the traffic had been heavy, the fifteen-minute journey back into town being time enough for him to calm down. They were in the CID room. Holmes was seated at his desk, hands clasped behind his head. Rebus was standing over him, breathing hard. On the desk sat a matt-black cassette deck.

Fahrt • sich zu beruhigen

verschränkt • schwer atmend

'Serial numbers match,' Holmes said, 'just in case you were wondering.'

stimmen überein

Rebus couldn't quite sound disinterested. 'How did you find him?'

With his hands still behind his head, Holmes managed a shrug. 'He was on file, sir. I just sat there flipping through them till I spotted him. That acne of his is as good as a tattoo. James Iain Bankhead, known to his friends as Jib. According to the file, you've arrested him a couple of times yourself in the past.'

und blätterte sie durch • entdeckte

laut

'Jib Bankhead?' said Rebus, as though trying to place the name. 'Yes, rings a bell.'

'I'd have thought it'd ring a whole fire station, sir. You

da klingelt was bei mir

Übung 45

Welche Wörter gehören zusammen?
Verbinden Sie sie mit einer Linie.

the lack of	footballer
to breathe	down
to ring	centre
a talented	someone's memory
a fifteen-minute	progress
to calm	hard
the city	a bell
to jog	journey

last arrested him three months ago.' Holmes made a show of consulting the file on his desk. 'Funny, you not recognising him …' Holmes kept his eyes on the file. 'I must be getting old,' Rebus said.

dass Sie ihn nicht wiedererkennen

Holmes looked up. 'So what now, sir?'

'Where is he?'

'Interview Room B.'

'Let him stay there then. Can't do any harm. Has he said anything?'

Kann nicht schaden.

'Not a word. Mind you, he *did* seem surprised when I paid him a visit.'

als ich ihm einen Besuch abstattete

'But he kept his mouth shut?'

Holmes nodded. 'So what now?' he repeated.

'Now,' said Rebus, 'you come along with me, Brian. I'll tell you all about it on the way …'

Wardle lived in a flat carved from a detached turn-of-the-century house on the south-east outskirts of the city. Rebus pressed the bell on the wall to the side of the substantial main door. After a moment, there was the muffled sound of footsteps, three clicks as locks were undone, and the door opened from within.

Wohnung • die abgeteilt war von • frei stehend • Vororte • beachtlich • gedämpft • Schlösser entriegelt wurden

'Good evening, Mr Wardle,' said Rebus. I see you're

Übung 46 Ordnen Sie die folgenden Begriffe den vier verschiedenen Bereichen zu. (clicks, keyhole, ground floor, moccasins, lock, flight of stairs, denims, voices, open-necked shirt, spy-hole, entrance hall, footsteps)

parts of a building
__________ __________
____

security-conscious at home at least.' Rebus was nodding towards the door, with its three separate keyholes, spy-hole and security chain.
'You can't be too – ' Wardle broke off as he saw what Brian Holmes was carrying. 'The deck!'
'Good as new,' said Rebus, 'apart from a few fingerprints.'
Wardle opened the door wide. 'Come in, come in.'
They entered a narrow entrance hall which led to a flight of stairs. Obviously the ground floor of the house did not belong to Wardle. He was dressed much as he had been in the shop: denims too young for his years, an open-necked shirt louder than a Wee Free sermon, and brown moccasins.
'I can't believe it,' he said, leading them towards the stairs. 'I really can't. But you could have brought it round to the shop …'
'Well, sir, we were going to be passing anyway.' Rebus closed the door, noting the steel plate on its inner face. The door-surround too was reinforced with metal plates. Wardle turned and noticed Rebus's interest.
'Wait till you see the hi-fi, Inspector. It'll all become clear.'

sicherheitsbewusst • Schlüssellöcher • Türspion • brach ab

abgesehen von

eng • Diele • Treppe • offensichtlich • gehörte … nicht • Jeans • mit offenem Kragen • bunter/lauter • presbyterianisch • Predigt

Stahl • Seite • Türrahmen • verstärkt

parts of a door

____
____
____

clothing

____
____
____

things that can be heard

__________ __________
____

	They could already hear the music. The bass was
Stufe •	vibrating each step of the stairs.
verständnisvoll	'You must have sympathetic neighbours,' Rebus remarked.
stocktaub	'She's ninety-two,' said Wardle. 'Deaf as a post. I went round to explain to her about the hi-fi just after I moved in. She couldn't hear a word I was saying.'
	They were at the top of the stairs now, where a smaller
Gang • offen	hallway led into a huge open-plan living-room and
angelegt •	kitchen. A sofa and two chairs had been pushed hard
nichts als •	back against one wall, and there was nothing but space
freier Platz •	between them and the opposite wall, where the hi-fi
gegenüber-	system sat, with large floor-standing speakers either
liegend • be-	side of it. One rack comprised half a dozen black boxes,
stand aus •	boasting nothing to Rebus's eye but a single red light.
rühmte sich •	'Amplifiers,' Wardle explained, turning down the
Verstärker	music.
	'What, all of them?'
Vorverstärker •	'Pre-amp and power supply, plus an amp for each driver.'
Netzteil •	Holmes had rested the cassette deck on the floor, but
Komponente •	Wardle moved it away immediately.
stört • Gerät	'Spoils the sound,' he said, 'if there's an extra piece of gear in the room.'

Übung 47 Ergänzen Sie die fehlenden Buchstaben der englischen Begriffe.

1. Mr Wardle's neighbour, a 92-year-old lady, was as __ e __ __ as a p __ __ __.
2. When Inspector Rebus and Sergeant Holmes went upstairs, they could feel the bass on each __ __ __ p.
3. The living-room and the __ i __ __ __ __ __ weren't separate rooms, but one big open-plan area.
4. There was a lot of __ __ __ c __ between the sofa and the hi-fi system.
5. Any extra piece of furniture would __ p __ __ __ the sound.

Holmes and Rebus stared at one another. Wardle was in his element now. 'Want to hear something? What's your taste?'
'Rolling Stones?' Rebus asked.
'*Sticky Fingers*, *Exile*, *Let It Bleed*?'
'That last one,' said Rebus.
Wardle went over to where a twenty-foot row of LPs was standing against the wall beneath the window.
'I thought those went out with the Ark,' said Holmes.
Wardle smiled. 'You mean with the CD. No, vinyl's still the best. Sit down.' He went over to the turntable and took off the LP he'd been playing. Rebus and Holmes sat. Holmes looked to Rebus, who nodded. Holmes got up again.
'Actually, could I use your loo?' he asked.
'First right out on the landing,' said Wardle. Holmes left the room. 'Any particular track, Inspector?'
'"Gimme Shelter",' stated Rebus. Wardle nodded agreement, set the needle on the disc, rose to his feet, and turned up the volume. 'Something to drink?' he asked. The room exploded into a wall of sound. Rebus had heard the phrase 'wall of sound' before. Well, here he was with his nose pressed against it.

Was ist Ihre Musikrichtung?

(1 Fuß = 30,48 cm) • unterhalb • wären vorsintflutlich • Plattenteller

Klo • Flur • Titel • nickte zustimmend • stand auf • Lautstärke

6. Most of the black boxes in Wardle's living-room were ___ ___ ___ l ___ f ___ ___ ___ ___.

7. When Inspector Rebus was asked about his ___ ___ s ___ ___ in music, he answered "Rolling Stones".

8. Wardle took off the record he had been playing and put a Rolling Stones LP on the ___ ___ r ___ t ___ b ___ ___.

9. When Rebus ___ o ___ ___ ___ d towards Sergeant Holmes, he got up and asked if he could use Wardle's bathroom.

10. After Wardle had given him directions, he went out onto the ___ ___ n ___ ___ ___ g.

11. When Wardle turned up the ___ o ___ ___ m ___, the whole room exploded into a wall of sound.

deutete mit dem Kopf • festgenagelt auf • außer • Oberfläche • obskure Dinge • Kunstdrucke • Tiefen • Krimskrams • geschieden • nagelneu • ansehnlich

'A whisky, please,' he yelled. Wardle tipped his head towards the hall. 'Same for him.' Wardle nodded and went off towards the kitchen area. Pinned to the sofa as he was, Rebus looked around the room. He had eyes for everything but the hi-fi. Not that there was much to see. A small coffee table whose surface seemed to be covered with arcana to do with the hi-fi system, cleaning-brushes and such like. There were some nice-looking prints on the wall. Actually, one looked like a real painting rather than a print: the surface of a swimming-pool, someone moving through the depths. But no TV, no shelves, no books, no knick-knacks, no family photos. Rebus knew Wardle was divorced. He also knew Wardle drove a Y-registered Porsche 911. He knew quite a lot about Wardle, but not yet enough …
A healthy glass of whisky was handed to him. Wardle placed another on the floor for Holmes, then returned to the kitchen and came back with a glass for himself. He sat down next to Rebus.
'What do you think?'
'Fantastic,' Rebus called back.
Wardle grinned.
'How much would this lot cost me?' Rebus asked, hop-

Übung 48 Bei verneinten Sätzen ist im Englischen im simple present und simple past eine do-Umschreibung nötig, wenn es sich um ein Vollverb handelt. Verwandeln Sie die folgenden positiven Sätze in negative Aussagesätze. Achten Sie dabei auf die Zeitform.

Beispiel: The print looked like a real painting.
The print didn't look like a real painting.

1. Inspector Rebus knew a lot about Wardle.

____

2. He likes classical music.

____

ing Wardle wouldn't notice how long Holmes had been out of the room.

'About twenty-five K.' — Tausend •

'You're joking. My flat didn't cost that.' — Sie machen Witze.

Wardle just laughed. But he was glancing towards the living-room door. He looked as though he might be about to say something, when the door opened and Holmes came in, rubbing his hands as though drying them off. He smiled, sat, and toasted Wardle with his glass. Wardle went over to the amplifier to turn down the volume. Holmes nodded towards Rebus. Rebus toasted no one in particular and finished his drink. The volume dipped.

prostete … zu

ließ nach

'What was that?' Holmes asked.

'*Let It Bleed.*'

'I thought my ears would.'

Wardle laughed. He seemed to be in a particularly good mood. Maybe it was because of the cassette deck.

Laune

'Listen,' he said, 'how the hell did you get that deck back so quickly?'

Holmes was about to say something, but Rebus beat him to it. 'It was abandoned.'

liegen gelassen

'Abandoned?'

3. Wardle sat down on the sofa.

____

4. The two detectives drink their whisky fast.

____

5. Holmes returned to the living-room immediately.

____

6. Wardle noticed that Sergeant Holmes had been gone for quite some time.

____

am Fuß

Wink • zusammengekniffen • schluckte … hinunter • Rabatt • im Gedächtnis behalten

'At the bottom of a flight of stairs on Queen Street,' Rebus went on. He had risen to his feet. Holmes took the hint and, eyes twisted shut, gulped down his whisky. 'So you see, sir, we were just lucky, that's all. Just lucky.' 'Well, thanks again,' said Wardle. 'If you ever want some hi-fi, drop into the shop. I'm sure a discount might be arranged.'

'We'll bear that in mind, sir,' said Rebus. 'Just don't expect me to put my flat on the market …'

sorgte … dafür, dass Jib freigelassen wurde • ausbreitete

Beute

gut bezahlt • die das Stehlen wert waren • entschärft • gesamt • hatten sich … ereignet

Back at the station, Rebus first of all had Jib released, then went to his office, where he spread the files out across his desk, while Holmes pulled over a chair. Then they both sat, reading aloud from lists. The lists were of stolen goods, high-quality stuff stolen in the dead of night by real professionals. The hauls – highly selective hauls – came from five addresses, the homes of well-paid middle-class people, people with things well worth the stealing.

Five robberies, all at dead of night, alarm systems disconnected. Art objects had been taken, antiques, in one case an entire collection of rare European stamps. The house-breakings had occurred at more or less

Übung 49 Welche der angegebenen Möglichkeiten ist die richtige? Kreuzen Sie sie an.

1. Inspector Rebus told Wardle that
- ☐ Sergeant Holmes had arrested the thief.
- ☐ the cassette deck had been left at the bottom of some steps.
- ☐ they had found the cassette deck in a stolen car.

2. There had been five similar robberies within the previous months.
- ☐ Great sums of money were stolen.
- ☐ Only jewellery was taken.
- ☐ Valuable collectors' items such as art objects and stamps were stolen.

monthly intervals, and all within a twenty-mile radius of central Edinburgh. The connection between them? Rebus had explained it to Holmes on their way to Wardle's flat.

'Nobody could see *any* connection, apart from the fact that the five victims worked in the west end. The Chief Super asked me to take a look. Guess what I found? They'd all had smart new hi-fi systems installed. Up to six months before the break-ins. Systems bought from Queensferry Audio and installed by Mr Wardle.'

'So he'd know what was in each house?' Holmes had said.

'And he'd be able to give the alarm system a look-over while he was there, too.'

'Could just be coincidence.'

'I know.'

Oh yes, Rebus knew. He knew he had only the hunch, the coincidence. He had no proof, no evidence of any kind. Certainly nothing that would gain him a search warrant, as the Chief Super had been good enough to confirm, knowing damned well that Rebus would take it further anyway. Not that this concerned the Chief Super, so long as Rebus worked alone, and didn't tell

Zeitabstände
Opfer • raten Sie • schick
zu inspizieren
Zufall
Ahnung • Beweis • Beweisstück • Durchsuchungsbefehl • bestätigen • interessierte

3. All the victims had one thing in common:
- They had bought an expensive hi-fi system from Mr Wardle's shop.
- They had all moved to Edinburgh within the previous six months.
- They were all members of the Scotch Malt Whisky Society.

4. Rebus suspected Wardle of
- having smuggled whisky.
- having claimed money for stolen items from the insurance.
- having checked the alarm systems in his customers' houses.

in der Schlinge • in Gefahr • Räumlichkeiten • Wachtmeister • vermeintlich • Unterhaltung • Ware • abgeschlossen • hatte … überredet • Kontrolleur • bevorzugt • Vorschlaghammer • wegzuspülen

his superiors what he was up to. That way, it was Rebus's neck in the noose, Rebus's pension on the line. Rebus guessed his only hope was that Wardle had kept some of the stolen pieces, that some of the stuff was still on his premises. He'd already had a young DC go into Queensferry Audio posing as a would-be buyer. The DC had gone in four times in all, once to buy some tapes, then to look at hi-fi, then to spend an hour in one of the demo rooms, and finally just for a friendly chat … He'd reported back to Rebus that the place was clean. No signs of any stolen merchandise, no locked rooms or cupboards …

So then Rebus had persuaded a uniformed constable to pose as a Neighbourhood Watch* supervisor. He had visited Wardle at home, not getting past the downstairs hallway. But he'd been able to report that the place was 'like Fort Knox*, metal door and all'. Rebus had had experience of steel-reinforced doors: they were favoured by drug dealers, so that when police came calling with a sledgehammer for invitation, the dealers would have time enough to flush everything away.

But a hi-fi dealer with a steel door … Well, that was a

info

Die **Neighbourhood Watch** ist eine ehrenamtliche Organisation, die der Polizei bei der örtlichen Verbrechensbekämpfung hilft, indem Mitglieder nach potenziellen Einbrechern und Autodieben Ausschau halten und während der Abwesenheit der Nachbarn auf deren Häuser aufpassen.

Im **Fort Knox**, einem Stützpunkt der US Army im Bundesstaat Kentucky, sind die Goldreserven der Vereinigten Staaten gelagert. Das Gebäude wurde aus Granit, Beton und verstärktem Stahl errichtet und ist durch eine 20 Tonnen schwere Tür gesichert.

new one. True, twenty-five grand's worth of hi-fi was an investment worth protecting. But there were limits. Not that Rebus suspected Wardle of actually doing the breaking and entering himself. No, he just passed the information on to the men Rebus really wanted, the gang. But Wardle was the only means of getting at them …

Finally, in desperation, Rebus had turned to Jib. And Jib had done what he was told, meaning Rebus now owed him a large favour. It was all highly irregular; unlawful, if it came to it. If anyone found out … well, Rebus would be making the acquaintance of his local broo office. Which was why, as he explained to Holmes, he'd been keeping so quiet about it.

The plan was simple. Jib would run off with something, anything, watched by Rebus to make sure nothing went wrong – such as a daring citizen's arrest by one or more passers-by. Later, Rebus would turn up at the shop to investigate the theft. Then later still, he would arrive at Wardle's flat, ostensibly to report the lack of progress. If a further visit was needed, the cassette deck would be found. But now he had Holmes's help, so one visit only should suffice, one man keeping

Riesen (Tausender) • verdächtigte • Einbruch

Mittel

aus Verzweiflung

ihm einen … Gefallen schuldete • ungesetzlich • Bekanntschaft • Arbeitsamt

wagemutig • Bürger • Diebstahl • angeblich

genügen

Welches der angegebenen Wörter passt in die Lücke?

Übung 50

1. A Detective Constable had been sent to find out if Wardle kept any stolen things on his ____________ in Queensferry Street.
- hallway
- hi-fi equipment
- premises

2. Inspector Rebus had asked Jib Bankhead to steal something from Wardle's shop, which was an ____________ thing to do.
- unlawful
- desperate
- effective

3. This is why Rebus knew that he owed Jib ____________.
- a favour
- some money
- an answer

herumschnüffelte	Wardle busy while the other sniffed around the rooms in the flat.
und studierten	They sat now, poring over the lists, trying to match what Holmes had seen in Wardle's two bedrooms with
als gestohlen gemeldet worden war • Reiseuhr	what had been reported stolen from the five luxury homes. 'Carriage clock,' read Rebus, 'nineteenth-century Japanese cigar box, seventeenth-century prints of Edinburgh by James Gordon, a Swarbreck lithograph…'
	Holmes shook his head at the mention of each, then read from one of his own lists. 'Ladies' and gents'
Erstausgabe	Longines watches, a Hockney print, Cartier pen, first-edition set of the Waverley novels, Ming vase, Dresden pieces… ' He looked up. 'Would you believe, there's
Kiste • Wert • Pfund • ich wette • Lager (Biersorte)	even a case of champagne.' He looked down again and read: 'Louis Roederer Cristal 1985. Value put at six hundred pounds. That's a hundred quid a bottle.' 'Bet you're glad you're a lager man,' said Rebus. He sighed. 'Does none of this mean anything to you, Brian?'
	Holmes shook his head. 'Nothing like any of this in either of the bedrooms.'

Übung 51 Welche Satzteile gehören zusammen?

Tragen Sie den entsprechenden Buchstaben in die Kästchen ein.

1. ☐ Inspector Rebus and Sergeant Holmes read out items from the lists of stolen things
2. ☐ There was a case of champagne on one of the lists
3. ☐ When Rebus saw the photo of a stolen print on a page from an art gallery's catalogue
4. ☐ As the print was part of a limited edition,
5. ☐ Although it had been a long day,
6. ☐ Sergeant Holmes wasn't sure what they would do if the print in Wardle's flat was not number forty-four.

Rebus cursed under his breath. 'Hold on,' he said. 'What about that print?'
'Which one? The Hockney?'
'Yes, have we got a photo of it?'
'Just this,' said Holmes, extracting from the file a page torn from an art gallery's catalogue. He handed it to Rebus, who studied the picture. 'Why?'
'Why?' echoed Rebus. 'Because you sat with this painting in front of your nose on Wardle's living-room wall. I thought it was a real painting, but this is it all right.' He tapped the sheet of paper. 'It says here the print's limited to fifty impressions. What number is the stolen one?'
Holmes looked down the list. 'Forty-four.'
'Right,' said Rebus. 'That should be easy enough to confirm.' He checked his watch. 'What time are you expected home?'
Holmes was shaking his head. 'Never mind that. If you're going back to Wardle's flat, I'm coming too.'
'Come on then.'
It was only as they were leaving the office that Holmes thought to ask: 'What if it isn't the same number on the print?'

cursed under his breath: fluchte • leise
extracting: und nahm heraus
torn from: herausgerissen aus
art gallery's: Kunstgalerie
impressions: Auflage von
are you expected: werden Sie ... erwartet

a) Sergeant Holmes decided not to go home, but to accompany Rebus to Wardle's flat again.
b) which was worth a hundred pounds per bottle.
c) it had a number on it.
d) He asked Rebus when they left the office.
e) he realized that it was exactly the one they had seen on a wall in Wardle's living-room.
f) and tried to remember whether they had seen anything of that sort in Wardle's flat.

'Then we'll just have to face the music,' said Rebus. But as it turned out, the only one facing the music was Wardle, and he sang beautifully. A pity, Rebus mused later, that he hadn't arranged for a discount on a new hi-fi system first. He'd just have to wait for Queensferry Audio's closing-down sale …

wie sich herausstellte • der singen musste • schade • Räumungsverkauf

Übung 52 Am Ende muss Inspector Rebus nur auf den Räumungsverkauf bei Queensferry Audio warten, um vielleicht doch noch an eine günstige Hifi-Anlage zu kommen. In dieser letzten Übung geht es um Ausdrücke mit sale bzw. sales. Verbinden Sie die englischen Begriffe mit der jeweils passenden deutschen Übersetzung.

sales pitch	Trödelmarkt
car-boot sale	Sommerschlussverkauf
sales slip	Totalausverkauf
saleroom	Verkaufsmasche
clearance sale	Kassenzettel
summer sales	Auktionsraum

Lösungen

1

1. T **Hamish MacDiarmid moderierte eine Radiosendung am Vormittag.**
2. F Viele Menschen hörten sich seine Sendung an, weil sie recht informativ war.
3. F Penny Cooks Anrufer waren aggressiv und lästig.
4. T **Penny gab ihnen Ratschläge, wenn sie ihr von ihren Problemen erzählten.**
5. F Inspector Rebus hörte Pennys Sendung jeden Abend an.
6. T **Er wusste nicht, wie Penny aussah.**

2

1. A **cheerful** person is someone who smiles and laughs a lot.
2. You use a **pad** to write notes.
3. Hamish MacDiarmid's **insults** (his rude and offensive remarks) did not keep people from calling.
4. Young girls often **giggle** when they think that something is funny or when they are nervous.
5. Penny Cook's hair was straight, but as she wanted it to be curly, she got it **permed**.

3

1. In order to get inside the radio station Inspector Rebus had to **pass through a combination-lock door**.
   Um in das Gebäude des Radiosenders zu kommen, musste Inspector Rebus durch eine Tür mit Kombinationsschloss gehen.

2. While he was passing studios and offices, Inspector Rebus could **hear the station's afternoon programme**.
   Während Inspector Rebus an Studios und Büros vorbeiging, konnte er das Nachmittagsprogramm des Senders hören.

3. The spiky-haired teenager who was talking to a middle-aged man in the corridor was **the singer of a band**.
   Der Teenager mit den spitz abstehenden Haaren, der im Gang mit einem Mann mittleren Alters sprach, war der Sänger einer Band.

4. Inspector Rebus had come for an interview with Penny Cook because **someone was threatening her**.
   Inspector Rebus war gekommen, um mit Penny Cook zu sprechen, weil jemand sie bedrohte.

4

1. Which of the following things is not to be found in Penny Cook's office? – **a phone box** (eine Telefonzelle)

2. Which of the following expressions has nothing to do with telephoning? – **sign up** (sich vormerken lassen)

3. Which word does not refer to a person? – a cassette player (ein Kassettenrekorder)

4. Which activity is not part of the call-in system at Lowland Radio? – Penny takes all the calls. (Penny nimmt alle Anrufe entgegen.)

5. Which of the following verbs is not a synonym of "think"? – descend (heruntergehen)

5 Schauplatz vieler Romane und Erzählungen von Ian Rankin

S C A R **E** D
N O **D**
L **I** G H T E R
G E N U I **N** E
B E E P
E R **U** P T
I N T E R **R** U P T
A N **G** E R
S **H** I V E R

6 1. d The crank caller tried to get through to Penny almost every night using different accents and dialects and giving different names and jobs.
Der Spaßanrufer versuchte fast jeden Abend, zu Penny durchzukommen, indem er unterschiedliche Akzente und Dialekte benutzte und unterschiedliche Namen und Berufe angab.

2. b When the anonymous caller knew that he had been found out, he shouted "I know what you've done!". Penny Cook had no idea what he might be referring to.
Wenn der anonyme Anrufer wusste, dass man ihn erkannt hatte, schrie er „Ich weiß, was Sie getan haben!". Penny Cook hatte keine Ahnung, worauf er anspielte.

3. e If they wanted to trace the caller, they had to keep him talking for some time.
Falls sie den Standort des Anrufers herausbekommen wollten, mussten sie ihn eine Weile in der Leitung halten.

4. f While the inspector was listening to the tape again, Penny got two cups of coffee.
Während sich der Inspektor das Band noch einmal anhörte, holte Penny zwei Becher Kaffee.

5. a Penny told Inspector Rebus that she did not make enemies and, looking at her and listening to her voice, he found that easy to believe.
Penny sagte Inspector Rebus, dass sie sich keine Feinde machte, und wenn er sie so ansah und ihre Stimme hörte, konnte er sich das gut vorstellen.

6. [c] Rebus suggested that other radio stations might be jealous of Penny's ratings, **but she just laughed at the idea that one of them might have hired someone to make the calls.**
Rebus brachte vor, dass andere Radiosender vielleicht neidisch auf Pennys Einschaltquoten waren, aber sie lachte nur bei dem Gedanken, dass einer von ihnen jemanden damit beauftragt haben könnte, die Anrufe zu machen.

7

1. Inspector Rebus couldn't talk to Sue. She was not in yet, because she was on **night shift** today.
2. As far as the ratings were concerned, Penny was still **ahead of** Hamish.
3. Penny Cook's show was mainly about the people who called in and about their **problems**.
4. Penny admitted that she was only **pretending** to have all the right answers to her callers' problems.
5. In order to find out what age groups listen to their shows radio stations have to do **market research**.
6. Inspector Rebus wanted to take the tape with him, so Penny **ejected** it.
7. The building was like a **maze** – there were so many corridors and doors that you could easily get lost.
8. Apart from hosting her show Penny had to answer piles of **fan mail**.

8

1. [F] Es war sehr laut auf dem Flur, als Inspector Rebus und Penny das Büro verließen.
2. [T] **Penny stellte Inspector Rebus ihren Chef und Hamish MacDiarmid vor.**
3. [F] Hamish MacDiarmid sah genauso aus, wie Inspector Rebus erwartet hatte.
4. [F] Gordon Prentice – Pennys Chef – trug einen grauen Anzug und ein weißes Hemd.
5. [T] **Gordon war ein gesund aussehender, ziemlich pummeliger Mann mit einem Bart und ziemlich vielen Haaren auf dem Kopf.**
6. [T] **Gordon Prentice hatte einen sehr festen Händedruck, MacDiarmids Griff war dagegen eher schwach.**
7. [T] **MacDiarmid schlug Gordon Prentice vor, dass Penny einen Tag seine Sendung übernehmen sollte und umgekehrt.**
8. [F] Penny gefiel die Idee, mit MacDiarmid die Sendungen zu tauschen.
9. [T] **MacDiarmid äußerte sich verächtlich über Pennys Zuhörer und nannte sie „soziale Krüppel".**
10. [T] **Penny hasste es, wenn MacDiarmid und Gordon Prentice sie zu ignorieren schienen.**

9

1. **publicity** shots
2. the call **of duty**
3. **a fifty-pence** refund
4. a jar **of coffee**
5. a promotional **gimmick**
6. **an ambiguous** look

10

1. Inspector Rebus was going to listen to Penny's show live at the radio station **the following evening.**
   Inspector Rebus hatte vor, Pennys Sendung am folgenden Abend live im Radiosender anzuhören.
2. If people want to make sure that no unwanted caller rings them, **they can keep their phone number ex-directory.**
   Wenn man sichergehen will, dass man keine ungewollten Anrufe bekommt, kann man im Telefonbuch keine Eintragung vornehmen lassen.
3. Inspector Rebus went to see someone who could **analyse the sound recording.**
   Inspector Rebus suchte jemanden auf, der die Aufnahme analysieren konnte.
4. Bill Costain didn't look and feel very well that morning because **he had celebrated his team's victory in a darts match the night before and had drunk too much alcohol.**
   Bill Costain sah an diesem Morgen nicht besonders gut aus und fühlte sich auch nicht so, weil er am Abend zuvor den Sieg seines Teams in einem Dart-Turnier gefeiert und zu viel getrunken hatte.

11

1. The anonymous caller was **disguising** his voice by speaking in a lower tone.
2. Inspector Rebus and Bill Costain used the **facilities** of a recording studio to retrieve the caller's real voice.
3. The radio at Rebus's office was still **tuned** to Lowland Radio.
4. Rebus **growled** when he heard the Camelot commercial again.

12

1. After the lunchtime peak the pub became a **quiet** place.
2. The barman **carefully** put the glasses onto the shelf behind the bar.
3. Rebus finished his drink **quickly**.
4. The young man was sitting at the table, **quietly** doing a crossword puzzle.
5. The ice-cube was **slowly** melting away in the glass of orange juice.
6. Rebus's voice was **confident** when he said: "I know what you've done."
7. As the man looked at Rebus **nervously**, the lock of hair fell forward again.
8. He threw a **quick** glance towards the door.
9. Rebus, who had obviously expected a **sudden** movement, grabbed the young man's arm and pulled him back.
10. "Sit down **immediately**!" Rebus ordered.

13

[1] Before her show Penny was a complete bundle of nerves.
Vor der Sendung war Penny ein Nervenbündel.

[2] She swallowed a small yellow tablet.
Sie schluckte eine kleine gelbe Tablette.

[3] The production team went through its paces.
Das Produktionsteam ging die einzelnen Schritte durch.

[4] Penny's microphone had to be replaced.
Pennys Mikrofon musste ersetzt werden.

[5] Penny wanted to know the order in which the musical pieces would be played.
Penny wollte die Reihenfolge wissen, in der die Musikstücke gespielt werden würden.

6 She winked at Inspector Rebus and crossed her fingers.
Sie zwinkerte Inspector Rebus zu und signalisierte „Daumen drücken“.
7 After the news the show’s theme music was played.
Nach den Nachrichten wurde die Titelmusik der Sendung gespielt.
8 The music faded and Penny went on the air.
Die Musik wurde langsam ausgeblendet und Penny ging auf Sendung.

14
1. At quarter to midnight Gordon Prentice came **into** the room.
2. Penny’s voice sounded as if it was apart **from** her.
3. Inspector Rebus looked **at** her **through** the large glass window.
4. The two operators scribbled **down** details **about** the callers.
5. “And now we’ve got Michael **on** line two.” Penny said.

15
1. agreeable, suitable, readable, ~~smile~~
2. discussion, protection, possession, ~~work~~

16

			1							
			a							
			s		2					
			h		c					
			a		o				3	
			m		n				b	
4	s	p	e	c	t	a	c	l	e	s
			d		r				a	
			5	c	a	s	t		m	
					r					
				6	y	e	l	l		

17
1. b When Inspector Rebus had listened to the Camelot coffee commercial once more, **he had suddenly realised that the voice of the man in the commercial and the voice of the anonymous caller were identical**.
Als Inspector Rebus den Werbespot für Camelot-Kaffee ein weiteres Mal gehört hatte, war ihm plötzlich bewusst geworden, dass die Stimme des Mannes im Werbespot und die Stimme des anonymen Anrufers identisch waren.

2. f In order to get the actor’s name and address Rebus **had contacted the ad agency**.
Um den Namen und die Adresse des Schauspielers zu bekommen, hatte Rebus die Werbeagentur kontaktiert.

3. c The young man Rebus had questioned at the wine bar was **Michael Barrie, an out-of-work actor**.
Der junge Mann, den Rebus in dem Weinlokal befragt hatte, war Michael Barrie, ein arbeitsloser Schauspieler.

4. [e] When Michael had called Penny at the station and threatened her, **he had thought that she knew about Gordon Prentice's plan**.
Als Michael Penny beim Sender angerufen und bedroht hatte, war er davon ausgegangen, dass sie über Gordon Prentices Plan Bescheid wusste.

5. [d] Penny shot a baleful glance in Prentice's direction, **before she told her listeners about what he had done**.
Penny warf Prentice einen unheilvollen Blick zu, bevor sie ihren Zuhörern mitteilte, was er getan hatte.

6. [a] After Gordon Prentice's manipulation of the phone-ins was discovered, **the radio station lost its licence and Penny Cook and Hamish MacDiarmid lost their jobs**.
Nachdem entdeckt worden war, wie Gordon Prentice die Anrufe manipuliert hatte, verlor der Radiosender seine Lizenz und Penny Cook und Hamish MacDiarmid verloren ihre Jobs.

18 [b] Nasenrücken: **bridge**
[c] Buchrücken: **spine**
[d] Handrücken: **back**
[a] Bergrücken: **ridge**

19 breath – **to breathe** – breathtaking
height – to heighten – high
danger – to endanger – **dangerous**
speaker – **to speak** – English-speaking
scare – to scare – **scary**
excitement – to excite – **excited (also: exciting)**

20 **1.** [F] Sir Walter Scott war durch eine Kugel getötet worden, die vom Schloss abgefeuert worden war.
2. [T] **Das Fernglas, das der Tote um den Hals hatte, war nagelneu.**
3. [T] **Er hatte einen Zettel erhalten, auf dem stand, dass er zur Spitze des Scott Monuments hinaufsteigen sollte.**
4. [F] Sergeant Holmes hatte den Zettel in Sir Walters Tasche gefunden.
5. [F] Inspector Rebus überließ dem Sergeant die Verantwortung dafür, die Leiche die Wendeltreppe hinunterzutransportieren.

21 **1.** If Sir Walter **hadn't climbed** up to the Monument, he wouldn't have died of a heart attack.
2. The guards might have noticed a suspicious person if there **hadn't been** so many tourists.
3. If people hadn't given Bobby food, he **wouldn't have survived**.

22 **1.** eagle **2.** heart **3.** gorgeous **4.** chest **5.** badge **6.** photographer **7.** peer **8.** accent

23

1. Rebus expected Superintendent Watson to be at the Scotts' house.
   He had seen Watson's car in the driveway.
   Rebus erwartete, dass Superintendent Watson im Haus der Scotts sein würde. Er hatte Watsons Auto in der Einfahrt stehen sehen.

2. The Superintendent wasn't very happy that Rebus had left Dr Jameson in charge of Sir Walter's dead body, **because the doctor wasn't very good at organising things**.
   Der Superintendent war nicht sehr glücklich darüber, dass Rebus Dr Jameson die Verantwortung für die Leiche Sir Walters überlassen hatte, weil der Doktor alles andere als ein Organisationsgenie war.

3. It was extremely difficult to move the dead body down the stairs because **the body was already stiff and got stuck in the spiral staircase**.
   Es war extrem schwierig, den Toten die Treppe hinunterzutransportieren, weil die Leichenstarre schon eingesetzt hatte und der steife Körper im spiralförmigen Treppenhaus stecken blieb.

4. The Scotts' living room was so big that it reminded Inspector Rebus of **a dance hall**.
   Das Wohnzimmer der Scotts war so groß, dass es Inspector Rebus an einen Tanzsaal erinnerte.

24

1. [c] Inspector Rebus had met Lady Scott before **when she had accompanied Sir Walter on several occasions**.
   Inspector Rebus war Lady Scott schon vorher begegnet, als sie Sir Walter bei mehreren Anlässen begleitet hatte.

2. [e] Quite a number of people had been put to prison by Sir Walter.
   One of them might have taken revenge and caused Sir Walter's death.
   Eine ganze Menge von Leuten waren von Sir Walter ins Gefängnis gebracht worden. Einer von ihnen könnte Rache genommen und Sir Walters Tod verursacht haben.

3. [f] Sir Walter's socks had become something of a trademark.
   He had only worn bright blue ones.
   Sir Walters Socken waren eine Art Markenzeichen geworden. Er hatte nur leuchtend blaue getragen.

4. [g] If you don't want to take a risk in a game of chess, **it is safer not to sacrifice the queen, but to play a pawn**.
   Wenn man bei einer Partie Schach nichts riskieren will, ist es sicherer, nicht die Dame zu opfern, sondern mit dem Bauern zu ziehen.

5. [a] Lady Scott was absolutely sure that her husband didn't own a pair of binoculars. **So he must have bought them on the morning before he went to the Scott Monument.**
   Lady Scott war absolut sicher, dass ihr Mann kein Fernglas besaß. Daher musste er es am Morgen gekauft haben, bevor er zum Scott-Denkmal ging.

6. d Lady Scott didn't know **where her husband was going on the day of his death**.
Lady Scott wusste nicht, wohin ihr Mann am Tag seines Todes ging.

7. b The note in the binocular case was not the only one.
Lady Scott had found some more in her husband's office.
Der Zettel in der Fernglashülle war nicht der Einzige. Lady Scott hatte einige weitere im Büro ihres Mannes gefunden.

25

1. Which of the following things could not be found in Sir Walter's office? – **a typewriter** (eine Schreibmaschine)
2. Where had Sir Walter kept the letters that he had received? – **in a folder** (in einer Mappe)
3. How did Lady Scott find the notes? – **She was looking for a particular newspaper.** (Sie suchte eine bestimmte Zeitung.)
4. What did Lady Scott not do after she had found the notes? – **She asked her husband what they meant.** (Sie fragte ihren Mann, was sie bedeuteten.)

26

1. Sir Walter **heard** from the blackmailer again.
2. In his second note he **told** Sir Walter that he **wanted** him to pay £ 2,000 for the embarrassing letters.
3. Sir Walter **got** the money from the bank and **put** it into a carrier bag.
4. Then he **went** to the Café Royal, **had** a drink at the bar and **left** the bag there.
5. When he **came** back a few minutes later, the money **was** gone, but he **found** the letters in the same place.
6. He **didn't see** the blackmailer, though.
7. At home he **looked** at the letters and **hid** them in his office.
8. But Sir Walter **didn't say** anything about the letters to his wife.

27

			2			3					
			l			i					
	1	d	o	u	b	t					
			w			i			5		
						n	4	p	a	g	e
			6	s	e	e	k		s		
						r			s		
7	i	n		c	h	a	r	g	e		
						r			n		
						y			t		

28 herd mentality
welcoming smile
pick up the telephone
package holiday

reception desk
deserted beach
laughing gas

29

1. When Inspector Rebus arrived at the Castellain Hotel, the receptionist **was talking** to someone on the phone.
2. While Rebus **was waiting** for the Grebe Tours representative, he **was watching** the tourists in the reception hall.
3. Rebus was **daydreaming** when he suddenly heard a man's voice saying "Hello!".

30

1. [T] **Tony Bell, der Vertreter von Grebe Tours, war ein kleiner Mann mit Bauchansatz.**
2. [T] **Als Tony Bell hörte, dass Rebus ein Polizeiinspektor war, war er ziemlich besorgt.**
3. [F] Ein Mitglied der Gruppe von Grebe Tours war ins Krankenhaus gebracht worden.
4. [T] **Die beiden Männer setzten ihre Unterhaltung in der Hotelbar fort.**
5. [F] In der Gruppe von Grebe Tours waren Leute aus Amerika, Kanada und Australien.
6. [F] Die Gruppe hatte Italien und Frankreich besucht, bevor sie nach Großbritannien kam.
7. [F] Während Rebus mit Tony Bell sprach, war die Gruppe gerade auf dem Rückweg von einem Ausflug in die Highlands.
8. [T] **Vor dem Abendessen fand ein Treffen statt, auf dem die Mitglieder der Gruppe über das Programm des folgenden Tages informiert wurden.**
9. [T] **Rebus beschloss, an dem Treffen teilzunehmen, da er einige Fragen stellen wollte.**
10. [F] Eine ältere Dame erzählte ihm, dass sie einen Inspektor von Scotland Yard kannte.
11. [F] Ein Taschendieb ist jemand, der in Häuser einbricht und Gegenstände stiehlt.

31

j	e	c	b	r	q	v	a	l	n	i	s
u	t	m	a	t	c	h	s	t	i	c	k
d	f	a	w	x	b	u	e	k	f	g	h
s	k	z	b	l	u	r	r	y	t	p	c
h	r	b	l	m	d	g	s	a	t	h	a
i	w	z	u	v	o	p	q	s	o	r	m
d	c	f	k	s	h	x	t	p	w	a	e
e	b	d	i	r	y	q	v	n	a	b	r
z	o	h	t	m	u	c	g	k	r	x	a
t	q	u	i	e	t	e	n	o	d	p	f
s	r	u	b	c	n	a	w	i	s	n	r
k	e	v	a	d	m	i	t	b	u	s	g

32
1. During the meeting Mrs Eglinton was sitting **in** the back row.
2. In a party of tourists there is always someone who complains **about** everything.
3. Inspector Rebus flipped **through** the photos which a member of the Grebe Tours party had taken.
4. Tony Bell told Rebus that the young man had been **on** holiday in Britain before.
5. His mother had died and **after** the funeral he decided to get away from all the sad memories.
6. He went into the travel agent's and booked a package tour **to** England and Scotland.
7. Sir Walter had withdrawn two thousand pounds **from** his bank accounts.
8. Inspector Rebus didn't know whether Sir Walter had got the letters **back**.
9. Lady Scott had looked **for** them in her husband's office, but hadn't found them.

33

vehicles	parts of the body	things in a room
cargo	palm	angle-poise
brakes	elbow	shelves
bus	knee	ashtray
tyres (= Reifen)	head	chair

34
1. Behind the row of books in the shelf there was enough **space** to hide the sheaf of letters.
2. The letters had been written with a **fountain pen**.
3. If someone had read the letters, this would have caused some **embarrassment** for Sir Walter.
4. Inspector Rebus didn't know whether the MP was still active in politics or whether he had already **retired**.

35

[1] Inspector Rebus wasn't sure what to do with the letters.
Inspector Rebus war sich nicht sicher, was er mit den Briefen tun sollte.

[2] He decided to put them back where he had found them.
Er entschloss sich, sie dorthin zurückzulegen, wo er sie gefunden hatte.

[3] Reaching down behind the line of books, he brushed against a stiff card.
Als er hinter die Reihe von Büchern griff, strich er gegen einen harten Karton.

[4] When he got it out, he saw that it was a photograph.
Als er ihn herausholte, sah er, dass es ein Foto war.

[5] It showed a man – Sir Walter in his thirties – and a woman with her arms wrapped around his.
Es zeigte einen Mann – Sir Walter, als er etwa Mitte dreißig war – und eine Frau, die ihre Arme um seine(n) geschlungen hatte.

[6] Rebus looked at the woman's face and suddenly realized where he had seen a face like hers before.
Rebus betrachtete das Gesicht der Frau und erkannte plötzlich, wo er ein solches Gesicht schon einmal gesehen hatte.

36 Superintendent Watson is Inspector Rebus'

			S	T	A	U	N	C	H
		C	U	R	S	E			
	A	P	P	E	A	R			
		H	E	A	L	T	H		
		U	R	G	E	N	T		
		L	I	E					
		S	O	I	L				
A	W	A	R	E					

37 **1.** Shaw Berkely, one of the Grebe Tours party, was **Sir Walter's son**.
Shaw Berkely, ein Mitglied der Gruppe von Grebe Tours, war Sir Walters Sohn.

2. Shaw Berkely wanted to take revenge on Sir Walter because **Sir Walter had made his mother unhappy**.
Shaw Berkely wollte sich an Sir Walter rächen, weil er seine Mutter unglücklich gemacht hatte.

3. The notes that Berkely sent to Sir Walter's house had been typed **before he set off to Britain**.
Die Zettel, die Berkely an Sir Walters Adresse schickte, waren getippt worden, bevor er nach Großbritannien aufbrach.

38

The doctor was in a jam. / fix. / tight spot.

39 **1.** What was the car like that Inspector Rebus was driving? – **It was rather old and shabby.** (Es war ziemlich alt und schäbig.)

2. Inspector Rebus said: "I've never been called to any sort of crime on this street." Which street is he referring to? – **Queensferry Street**

3. Why had Detective Sergeant Holmes come with Inspector Rebus? – **He didn't feel like doing paperwork in the office.** (Er hatte keine Lust auf Schreibtischarbeit im Büro.)

40 **1.** engine – windscreen – ~~yell~~ – steering wheel
Alle anderen Wörter beziehen sich auf Teile eines Autos.

2. dead end – ~~fault~~ – pedestrian passage – traffic lights
Alle anderen Begriffe beziehen sich auf Straßen und Straßenverkehr.

3. to leap – to sprint – to walk – ~~to agree~~
Alle anderen Wörter sind Verben der Fortbewegung.

4. ~~narrow~~ – calmly – carefully – loudly
Alle anderen Wörter sind Adverbien und bringen zum Ausdruck, wie jemand etwas tut.

5. to wave – to point – ~~to step~~ – to flap
Alle anderen Bewegungen macht man mit den Armen.

41 someone who steals things: **thief**
to get more points in a game or competition: **to beat someone**
to make something stop moving: **to pull to a halt**
the vehicles moving along a street: **traffic**
to have the same opinion about something: **to agree**
to change directions: **to turn**

42
1. A CD shelf **had been knocked over by the thief.**
2. A description of the thief **was given to Inspector Rebus by some passers-by.**
3. A murder **was committed last night.**
4. A specialist **has been sent to the scene of the crime.**

43

				1											
				i				2				3			
				n				s				f			
				f				p				o			
	5	l	o	u	d	s	p	e	a	k	e	r	s		
				r				c				m			
6	c	h	a	i	n			k						4	
				a		7	f	l	a	m	m	a	b	l	e
				t				e						a	
				e				d						d	

44
1. T **Sergeant Holmes war so wütend über einen Jungen in seiner Fußballmannschaft gewesen, dass er ihn zu Fall gebracht hatte.**
2. F Inspector Rebus wies Holmes an, die Akten der jugendlichen Straftäter zu überprüfen.
3. T **Holmes entdeckte den Jungen, der das Kassettendeck gestohlen hatte, in den Akten.**
4. T **Inspector Rebus hatte Jib Bankhead mehrere Male verhaftet.**
5. F Rebus war außerordentlich zufrieden darüber, dass Sergeant Holmes den Dieb gefunden hatte.

45 the lack of progress
to breathe hard
to ring a bell
a talented footballer
a fifteen-minute journey
to calm down
the city centre
to jog someone's memory

46

parts of a building	**parts of a door**
ground floor	keyhole
flight of stairs	lock
entrance hall	spy-hole

clothing	things that can be heard
moccasins	clicks
denims	voices
open-necked shirt	footsteps

47

1. Mr Wardle's neighbour, a 92-year-old lady, was as **deaf** as a **post**.
2. When Inspector Rebus and Sergeant Holmes went upstairs, they could feel the bass on each **step**.
3. The living-room and the **kitchen** weren't separate rooms, but one big open-plan area.
4. There was a lot of **space** between the sofa and the hi-fi system.
5. Any extra piece of furniture would **spoil** the sound.
6. Most of the black boxes in Wardle's living-room were **amplifiers**.
7. When Inspector Rebus was asked about his **taste** in music, he answered "Rolling Stones".
8. Wardle took off the record he had been playing and put a Rolling Stones LP on the **turntable**.
9. When Rebus **nodded** towards Sergeant Holmes, he got up and asked if he could use Wardle's bathroom.
10. After Wardle had given him directions, he went out onto the **landing**.
11. When Wardle turned up the **volume**, the whole room exploded into a wall of sound.

48

1. Inspector Rebus **didn't know** a lot about Wardle.
2. He **doesn't like** classical music.
3. Wardle **didn't sit** down on the sofa.
4. The two detectives **don't drink** their whisky fast.
5. Holmes **didn't return** to the living-room immediately.
6. Wardle **didn't notice** that Sergeant Holmes had been gone for quite some time.

49

1. Inspector Rebus told Wardle **that the cassette deck had been left at the bottom of some steps**.
   Inspector Rebus teilte Wardle mit, dass das Kassettendeck am Fuß einer Treppe zurückgelassen worden war.

2. There had been five similar robberies within the previous months. **Valuable collectors' items such as art objects and stamps were stolen.**
   Innerhalb der vorangegangenen Monate hatte es fünf ähnliche Diebstähle gegeben. Wertvolle Sammlerstücke wie Kunstgegenstände und Briefmarken waren gestohlen worden.

3. All the victims had one thing in common:
   They had bought an expensive hi-fi system from Mr Wardle's shop.
   Alle Opfer hatten eines gemeinsam: Sie hatten in Herrn Wardles Geschäft eine teure Hifi-Anlage gekauft.

4. Rebus suspected Wardle of **having checked the alarm systems in his customers' houses**.

Rebus verdächtigte Wardle, die Alarmanlagen in den Häusern seiner Kunden inspiziert zu haben.

50 1. A Detective Constable had been sent to find out if Wardle kept any stolen things on his **premises** in Queensferry Street.
2. Inspector Rebus had asked Jib Bankhead to steal something from Wardle's shop, which was an **unlawful** thing to do.
3. This is why Rebus knew that he owed Jib **a favour**.

51 1. [f] Inspector Rebus and Sergeant Holmes read out items from the lists of stolen things **and tried to remember whether they had seen anything of that sort in Wardle's flat.**
Inspector Rebus und Sergeant Holmes lasen die Dinge von der Liste gestohlener Gegenstände vor und versuchten, sich daran zu erinnern, ob sie irgendetwas davon in Wardles Wohnung gesehen hatten.

2. [b] There was a case of champagne on one of the lists **which was worth a hundred pounds per bottle.**
Auf einer der Listen war eine Kiste Champagner, der hundert Pfund pro Flasche wert war.

3. [e] When Rebus saw the photo of a stolen print on a page from an art gallery's catalogue **he realized that it was exactly the one they had seen on a wall in Wardle's living-room.**
Als Rebus auf einer Seite aus dem Katalog einer Kunstgalerie das Foto eines gestohlenen Kunstdrucks sah, erkannte er, dass es genau derselbe war, den er an der Wand von Wardles Wohnzimmer gesehen hatte.

4. [c] As the print was part of a limited edition, **it had a number on it.**
Da der Druck Teil einer limitierten Auflage war, hatte er eine Nummer.

5. [a] Although it had been a long day, **Sergeant Holmes decided not to go home, but to accompany Rebus to Wardle's flat again.**
Obwohl es ein langer Tag gewesen war, beschloss Sergeant Holmes, nicht nach Hause zu gehen, sondern Rebus noch einmal zu Wardles Wohnung zu begleiten.

6. [d] Sergeant Holmes wasn't sure what they would do if the print in Wardle's flat was not number forty-four. **He asked Rebus when they left the office.**
Sergeant Holmes war sich nicht sicher, was sie tun würden, wenn der Druck in Wardles Wohnung nicht Nummer 44 war. Er fragte Rebus, als sie das Büro verließen.

52

sales pitch	Verkaufsmasche
car-boot sale	Trödelmarkt
sales slip	Kassenzettel
saleroom	Auktionsraum
clearance sale	Totalausverkauf
summer sales	Sommerschlussverkauf

Wörterverzeichnis

A

abandoned liegen gelassen
above über
abrasive ruppig
access Zugang
to accompany begleiten
according to laut
account Konto
to ache wehtun, Schmerzen haben
to achieve hervorbringen
a couple of einige
acquaintance Bekanntschaft
actress Schauspielerin
actually tatsächlich
to address someone zu jemandem sprechen
to admit einräumen
adultery Ehebruch
adversary Feind(in)
advert Werbespot
advertiser Werbekunde, Werbekundin
advice Ratschlag
affair Sache
to affect something sich auf etwas auswirken
to agree zustimmen
ahead of vor
air brake Druckluftbremse
albeit wenn auch
ambiguous mehrdeutig
ambulanceman Sanitäter
amplifier Verstärker
anger Wut, Groll
to angle ausrichten
angle-poise Gelenklampe
to announce erklären
antiquated veraltet
Any joy? Glück gehabt?
apparently offenbar
apart from abgesehen von; getrennt von
to appeal to eine Anziehungskraft ausüben auf
to appear erscheinen
to approach sich nähern, näher kommen
appropriately entsprechend
arcana obskure Dinge
Ark Arche Noah
art gallery Kunstgalerie
to ascertain herausfinden, feststellen
ashtray Aschenbecher
assent Zustimmung
to assess beurteilen
to assure versichern
as though als ob
to attach anbringen, anheften
at the bottom am Fuß
attitude Einstellung
at your service zu Ihren Diensten
available verfügbar

award Preis, Auszeichnung
aware bewusst
awe Ehrfurcht
awkward unbeholfen; peinlich
aye ja

B

background Hintergrund
back row letzte Reihe
badge Plakette
to baffle verblüffen
baggy ausgebeult, weit
balding mit schütter werdendem Haar
baleful unheilvoll
bank executive Bankdirektor(in)
barely kaum
bargain Geschäft; Angebot
barred ausgeschlossen, versperrt
base Standort
basically im Wesentlichen, im Grunde genommen
battle Schlacht
not to be (was/were – been) able to organise a brewery visit nichts auf die Reihe kriegen
to be about to do something im Begriff sein, etwas zu tun
beaker Becher
beam Strahl
to bear (bore – borne) tragen
to bear in mind im Gedächtnis behalten
to bear with someone Geduld mit jemandem haben
to be ashamed sich schämen
to beat (beat – beaten) schlagen
to be connected verbunden werden
to be eagle-eyed aufmerksam sein; Adleraugen haben
beefy pummelig
beep Piepton
to be fed up with die Nase voll haben von
not to be forthcoming ausbleiben
to be found out entdeckt werden
to be hard on someone zu jemandem gemein sein
to be honest ehrlich gesagt
to be in charge of verantwortlich sein für
to be keen on auf etwas erpicht/scharf sein
to belong to gehören (zu)
beneath unterhalb, unter
to be on the line in Gefahr sein
to be out of something etwas nicht mehr (vorrätig) haben
to be resting ohne Engagement sein
to be said to be gelten als
to best übertreffen
to be stuck feststecken, festgeklemmt sein
to be supposed to do something etwas tun sollen
to bet (bet – bet) wetten
to be taken ill erkranken
to be up to something etwas im Schilde führen
beyond the call of duty weit mehr als nur Pflichterfüllung
bigoted selbstgerecht, bigott
binoculars Fernglas
to bite (bit – bitten) schneiden; beißen
blackmail Erpressung

blank charge Böllerschuss
blessed verflixt
to blink blinzeln
blurry verschwommen
to boast sich rühmen
booking Buchung
to boost steigern
to bother sich die Mühe machen, sich kümmern
to bounce off reflektieren
bow Verbeugung
bowed gesenkt
to break (broke – broken) off abbrechen
to break a duck eine Tradition brechen
breaker's yard Schrottplatz
breaking and entering Einbruch
to breathe atmen
breathless atemlos
breathtaking atemberaubend
bridge (Nasen-)Rücken
bright leuchtend
brisk forsch
brittle zerbrechlich
broad breit
to broadcast ausstrahlen
broo office Arbeitsamt
to brush streichen
bugger Kerl
to bulge sich ausbeulen
bull Stier
to burst (burst – burst) through durchbrechen, sich durchzwängen
busy beschäftigt
but außer
buxom drall
by accident durch Zufall
by chance zufällig
by dint of durch
by-line Seitenlinie

C

ca' canny sei vorsichtig
cage Käfig
calculator Taschenrechner; Rechenmaschine
call Anruf
callous kaltschnäuzig
to calm down sich beruhigen
to career rasen
cargo Fracht
carriage clock Reiseuhr
carrier bag Tragetüte
to carve abteilen
case Hülle; Kiste
cash Bargeld
cast Besetzung
to cast (cast – cast) an eye einen Blick werfen
to catch (caught – caught) up on something etwas nachholen, abarbeiten
ceiling (Zimmer-)Decke
century Jahrhundert
chain Kette
challenge Herausforderung
challenger Herausforderer
charge Schützling
chat Unterhaltung
cheerful fröhlich
chess Schach
chest Brust
chickpeas Kichererbsen
chief superintendent Kriminalhauptkommissar(in)

chin Kinn
to choose (chose – chosen) aussuchen
to chuckle schmunzeln
CID (= Criminal Investigation Department) Kriminalpolizei
citizen Bürger(in)
to clasp umfassen, umklammern, verschränken
clockwork Uhrwerk
closing-down sale Räumungsverkauf
closing-time Sperrstunde
cloying übermäßig süß
to clutch umklammern
cluttered überhäuft
coincidence Zufall
colon Doppelpunkt
combative streitlustig
combination lock Kombinationsschloss
to come (came – come) across something auf etwas stoßen
to come forth (hervor)kommen
to come in handy praktisch sein
comfortable bequem
commercial Werbespot
to commit a crime ein Verbrechen begehen
common gewöhnlich
common knowledge allgemein bekannt
compartment Fach
to complain sich beschweren
to comprise bestehen aus
concerned betroffen
concerning betreffend
to concern someone jemanden interessieren
concertina Ziehharmonika
concise knapp und präzise
condiment Würzmittel
confidently selbstsicher
to confirm bestätigen
conjecture Mutmaßen, Vermutung
connection Anschluss(flug)
to consist of bestehen aus
conspicuous auffällig
copious reichlich
copper Bulle (Polizist)
corpse Leiche
counselling Beratung
to counter kontern, parieren
courtroom Gerichtssaal
cover Tarnung
to crackle knistern
cramped eng
crank Spinner
crank call Telefonstreich, Spaßanruf
crawl Schneckentempo
cripple Krüppel
croft Cottage in den schottischen Highlands
cropped hair Igelhaarschnitt
to crop up (plötzlich) auftauchen
crossword clue Kreuzworträtselfrage
to crouch kauern, hocken
crowded überfüllt
crucial entscheidend
to crunch kauen, zermalmen
cupped hohl
curse Fluch
to curse verfluchen, fluchen
to cuss fluchen
to cut (cut – cut) someone off jemandem den Weg abschneiden

D

to dab tupfen
damage Beschädigung
daring wagemutig
dazed benommen
DC (= Detective Constable) Kriminalwachtmeister(in)
dead end Sackgasse
deaf as a post stocktaub
dealer Händler(in)
to deal (dealt – dealt) with something sich um etwas kümmern, sich einer Sache annehmen
dear teuer
decade Jahrzehnt
to deduce folgern
delay Verzögerung
delicate zierlich
to deliver abliefern
demanding anstrengend
to demur Einwände erheben
denims Jeans
depressing bedrückend
depth Tiefe
deranged verwirrt, verstört
to descend heruntergehen
description Beschreibung
deserted menschenleer
desperation Verzweiflung
despite trotz
despite himself widerwillig
to destroy vernichten
detached house frei stehendes Haus
to deter abhalten
devious verschlagen
diddle Schwindel
to dig herumwühlen
digit Ziffer, Zahl
dignified würdevoll
to diminish (sich) abschwächen
dimly vage
dimly lit schwach beleuchtet
to dip abfallen
disbelieving ungläubig
to discard someone jemanden fallen lassen
to disconnect entschärfen, unterbrechen
discount Rabatt
to discover entdecken
to disguise verschleiern, verstellen
dishevelled zerzaust
to dish out austeilen
display Sammlung
to disturb beunruhigen
disturbed verwischt
divorced geschieden
to do (did – done) a circuit of something um etwas herumfahren
to do a runner zu Fuß fliehen
to do a three-point-turn in drei Zügen wenden
to dodge ausweichen
doomsday Tag des Jüngsten Gerichts
door-surround Türrahmen
to do the Grand-Slam im Rugby-Turnier Six Nations alle Gegner besiegen
to double over zusammenbrechen
doubt Zweifel
to doubt bezweifeln
dozen Dutzend
to draw (drew, drawn) ziehen
to draw a blank keinen Einfall haben
drawer Schublade

drawn langgezogen
drivel Gefasel
driver Komponente, Einzelgerät
drop Abhang, Abfall; Höhenunterschied
to drop someone jemanden absetzen
due fällig
dull grau
duty Verpflichtung

E

edge Rand, Kante; Klang (in der Stimme)
editor Herausgeber(in), Redakteur(in)
efficient tüchtig
either side auf beiden Seiten
to eject auswerfen
elaborate raffiniert
elbow Ellbogen
elderly älter
embarrassing peinlich
embarrassment Peinlichkeit
to emerge herauskommen
employed beschäftigt
to enclose beifügen
to encourage bestärken
engine Motor
engineer Techniker(in)
en route auf dem Weg
entire gesamt
entrance hall Diele
to erupt hervorbrechen, laut werden
esplanade Promenade
ethereal ätherisch
eventually schließlich
evidence Beweisstück
to exact erzwingen
to exaggerate übertreiben
exaggeration Übertreibung
to examine begutachten
except nur, dass; außer
exchange Austausch
excited erregt, aufgeregt
excuse Vorwand
ex-directory nicht im Telefonbuch eingetragen
to exit weggehen, verschwinden
to expect erwarten
expensive teuer
expression Ausdruck
to extract herausnehmen

F

face Seite, Fläche
to face the music für etwas geradestehen, auspacken, singen
facilities Geräte
factual sachlich
to fade verklingen, leiser werden
faint schwach
fairly ziemlich, geradezu
to fancy Lust haben auf
fancy seeing you here so was, Sie hier zu sehen
farther weiter
fault Schuld
favour Gefallen
to favour bevorzugen
feasible machbar
felt tip Filzstift
to fend off abwehren
ferocious wütend
fervour Eifer
few wenige
fierce heftig

file Akte
to finalise endgültig festlegen
firm fest
first edition Erstausgabe
fix abgekartetes Spiel
to fix on richten auf
to flake abblättern
flammable leicht entzündbar
to flap one's arms mit den Armen wedeln
flash Blitz
flat Wohnung
fleck Spritzer
to flee (fled – fled) fliehen
to flesh out deutlich machen
to flick schnipsen, streichen
flight of stairs Treppe
to flip umlegen
to flip through something etwas durchblättern
to flush away wegspülen
to focus konzentriert schauen
focused scharf eingestellt
to fold one's arms die Arme verschränken
to follow suit dem Beispiel folgen
foot Fuß (Längenmaß, 1 Fuß = 30,48 cm)
for a change zur Abwechslung
to force-feed (force-fed – force-fed) zwangsweise verabreichen
forecourt Vorplatz
forefinger Zeigefinger
for emphasis um dem ganzen Nachdruck zu verleihen
forensic science lab kriminaltechnisches Labor
form Formular
for our benefit only nur für uns
for the umpteenth time zum x-ten Mal
to fortify stärken
for which relief much thanks worüber ich sehr erleichtert bin
fountain pen Füllfederhalter
to fret sich aufregen
to frown die Stirn runzeln
frozen (wie) eingefroren
to fume vor Wut rauchen
funeral Beerdigung

G

gap Lücke
gatekeeper Wache, Pförtner(in)
to gather einsammeln
gear Gerät, Teil
genuine aufrichtig, echt
to get (got – got) fed up with something an etwas die Lust verlieren
to get to someone jemandem auf den Geist gehen
gift Gabe
to giggle kichern
to give (gave – given) someone a bell jemanden anrufen
to give something a look-over etwas inspizieren
to glance at einen Blick werfen auf
to glance through something etwas flüchtig durchsehen
glowing glühend
to goad reizen
gob Schnauze
to go (went – gone) dead zum Stillstand kommen
to go freelance freiberuflich arbeiten

to go out with the Ark vorsintflutlich sein
gorgeous hinreißend
graft Schinderei
grain of Quäntchen
grand Riese, Tausender
greedy ballverliebt
to greet grüßen
grim düster
to grin grinsen
growl Brummen
to growl knurren
to guess raten
guide Reiseführer(in)
to gulp down hinunterschlucken
gust of wind Windböe
guy Kerl, Typ

H

hallway Gang
hand Uhrzeiger
to hand over aushändigen
handkerchief Taschentuch
handy praktisch
hard schwer
hardly kaum
hard-pressed gestresst
harm Schaden
harrassed gestresst
hassle Theater
haul Beute
haunt Stammlokal
to have (had – had) a bend in one's tackle einen Sprung in der Schüssel haben
to have an objection einen Einwand haben
health Gesundheit
healthy gesund; ansehnlich
heart attack Herzinfarkt
he doesn't mind es macht ihm nichts aus
height Gipfel
to heighten erhöhen
hell verdammt
hemline Saum
hence daher
herd mentality Herdentrieb
here's to ... auf ... *Trinkspruch*
to hide (hid – hidden) sich verstecken
hint Hauch; Wink
hiss Rauschen
to hiss zischen
to hog the ball den Ball nicht abgeben
hooker Nutte
to host moderieren
housing scheme Wohnsiedlung
to hug umarmen
humiliation Demütigung
hunch Ahnung
hurt verletzt
hushed gedämpft, leise
husky rau

I

imagery Bildersprache
immediately unmittelbar; sofort
impression Eindruck; Auflage
inadvertently unbeabsichtigterweise
inch Längenmaß (1 Inch = 2,54 cm)
incline Anstieg
incriminating belastend
in disbelief ungläubig

in embarrassment verlegen
infamous berüchtigt
in favour of zu Gunsten von
infirm schwach
inflamed entbrannt
to infuriate wütend machen
in mitigation zur Verteidigung
innocuous harmlos
in search of auf die/der Suche nach
insecure unsicher
instead stattdessen
insult Beleidigung
insurance Versicherung
intake Ladung
intent on konzentriert auf
to intercept abhören
interchange Wortwechsel
interlude Zwischenprogramm
to interrupt anhalten, unterbrechen
interval Zeitabstand
in the first place überhaupt erst
intrigued fasziniert
to intrude on someone jemanden belästigen, stören
to investigate nachsehen, ermitteln
investigation Ermittlung
involved beteiligt
item Gegenstand
itinerary Reiseroute
it's a living es hält mich über Wasser
it's a pity schade

J

jar Glas
to jink sich schlängeln, Ausweichmanöver machen
to jog auf die Sprünge helfen
joint gemeinsam
to joke Witze machen
journey Fahrt
joust Zweikampf
to judge by something nach etwas urteilen
judicious klug
juicy interessant

K

K Tausend
to keep (kept – kept) doing something immer wieder/weiter machen
keyhole Schlüsselloch
to kill two birds zwei Fliegen mit einer Klappe schlagen
knick-knack Krimskrams
knighthood Adelstitel
knowledge Wissen

L

lack of Fehlen von, Mangel an
lad Junge
lager Lager *Biersorte*
landing Flur
land of Nod Reich der Träume
lap Schoß
lapel Revers
larder Speiseschrank
to last anhalten
to late-bloom spät blühen
to lay (laid – laid) down festlegen, aufstellen, stellen
to lead (led – led) the way vorausgehen
to lean on sich lehnen an
to leap (leapt – leapt) out hinausspringen

to leave (left – left) someone in the lurch jemanden hängen lassen
ledge Ablage
legend Schriftzug
lethal tödlich
lighter Feuerzeug
limp schlaff
to linger länger verweilen
liquid Flüssigkeit; flüssig, feucht
lock Schloss
locked abgeschlossen
to lock one's arms around someone jemanden festhalten, packen
loo Klo
loot Knete
loud bunt; laut
loudspeaker Lautsprecher
low gedämpft, leise
to lower senken
lukewarm lauwarm
lunatic Verrückter

M

to make (made – made) sense Sinn ergeben
to manage to do something schaffen, etwas zu tun
manilla envelope brauner Umschlag
market research Marktforschung
to marvel at something über etwas staunen
to match übereinstimmen
to match to in Einklang bringen mit
matchstick Streichholz
mauled beschädigt
maze Labyrinth
to mean (meant – meant) bedeuten
means Mittel
meantime in der Zwischenzeit
merchandise Ware
merely bloß
mike Mikro(fon)
to mill around umherlaufen
mind wissen Sie
mind you wohlgemerkt
mint Pfefferminzbonbon
misery Leid
money belt Gürteltasche
mood Laune
to mother bemuttern
mottled fleckig
mould Form, Kontur
to mount befestigen
mourning Trauer
to mouth überdeutlich sagen
muffled gedämpft
mugger Straßenräuber
to mull grübeln
to muse sinnieren
musty muffig
to mutter brummeln, murmeln
my heart sinks meine Stimmung verschlechtert sich; mich verlässt der Mut

N

namesake Namensvetter
narrow eng
neat gepflegt
neck Hals
neither keiner (von beiden)
nevertheless trotzdem
night shift Nachtschicht
to nip kneifen

to nod nicken
to nod agreement zustimmend nicken
none keiner, keine
noose Schlinge
note Notiz
nothing but nichts als
numb gefühllos
numerous zahlreich
nut Verrückter

O

obligation Pflicht
obstruction Behinderung
obvious naheliegend
obviously offensichtlich
occupant Gast
to occur sich ereignen
odd gelegentlich
off neben
offender Straftäter(in)
to offset (offset – offset) aufwiegen
on-air auf Sendung
oncoming traffic Gegenverkehr
on the broo arbeitslos
on the contrary im Gegenteil
on the go aktiv
on the q.t. heimlich
open-necked mit offenem Kragen
open-plan durchgehend
opposite gegenüberliegend
ornate kunstvoll
ostensibly angeblich
out of earshot außer Hörweite
out of work arbeitslos
to outpace someone jemanden abhängen
outskirts Stadtrand
to outstare someone jemanden übertreffen
overcast trüb(sinnig), bewölkt
over the odds zu viel
to owe verdanken
to owe someone a favour jemandem einen Gefallen schulden

P

pace Schritt
to pace auf und ab gehen
package company Pauschalreise-veranstalter
package holiday Pauschalurlaub
pad Block
to page someone jemanden ausrufen lassen
paisley-patterned mit Paisleymuster
palm Handfläche
to paper-clip mit einer Büroklammer befestigen
parapet Brüstung
to pardon entschuldigen
parental elterlich
particular speziell
party Gruppe
passer-by Passant(in)
to pat tätscheln, klopfen
paunch Bauch
pawn Bauer
to pay (paid – paid) someone a visit jemandem einen Besuch abstatten
payoff Bezahlung; Übergabe
to pay up bezahlen
peak Spitze; Stoßzeit
pedestrian Fußgänger(in)
to peel something away etwas ablösen
to peer schauen, spähen

pensive nachdenklich
permed dauergewellt
to persist anhalten, weitergehen
to persuade überreden
pickpocket Taschendieb
pinball Flipper
pinned festgenagelt
pitch Tonhöhe
pity Mitleid
to placate besänftigen
plaque Gedenktafel
to play up verrückt spielen
to plead inständig flehen
pleased erfreut
point Sinn; Punkt
to point zeigen, deuten
points system Punktesystem
polaroid Sofortbildkamera
polythene bag Plastiktüte
pool Pool-Billard
to pop out kurz weggehen
to pop something into one's mouth sich etwas in den Mund stecken
to pore over genau studieren
to possess in Besitz haben, besitzen
potion Zaubertrank
pot-planted mit Kübelpflanzen versehen
power of attraction Anziehungskraft
power supply Netzteil
practice Training
pre-amp(lifier) Vorverstärker
pregnant schwanger
premises Räumlichkeiten
present company excluded Anwesende ausgeschlossen
presumably vermutlich
to presume vermuten
to pretend vorgeben, so tun als ob
to prevent verhindern
print Foto, Abzug; Kunstdruck
pro Profi
probably vermutlich
production line Fließband
progress Fortschritt(e)
promotional gimmick Werbegag
proof Beweis
proprietor Besitzer(in)
to prosper zu Wohlstand gelangen
protection racket Schutzgelderpressung
protestation Protesterklärung
to protrude hervorquellen
to provide zur Verfügung stellen
to pry herumschnüffeln
public öffentlich
publicity shot PR-Foto
to pull to a halt anhalten
to pump someone's hand jemandem die Hand fast abschütteln
punch-drunk verbeult
purpose Zweck
to purse one's lips die Lippen zusammenpressen
push-button array Tastenfeld
to put (put – put) a trace on someone jemandes Anrufe zurückverfolgen lassen
put-on verstellt
to put one's foot down Gas geben
to put out a contract on someone jemanden auf eine Person ansetzen
to put someone behind bars jemanden hinter Gitter bringen
puzzled verwirrt

Q

QC (Queen's Council) Kronanwalt, Kronanwältin
quarry Beute
quid Pfund
to quieten zur Ruhe/zum Schweigen bringen
quite ganz
to quote zitieren

R

rack component Teil einer Stereoanlage
radio Funkgerät
rage Wut
raging wütend
rail Fußleiste
to raise (hoch-)heben
ramification Auswirkung
rampart Festungswall
ram-raider Einbrecher, der ein Schaufenster mit dem Auto auframmt
rank Dienstrang
rather lieber
ratings Einschaltquoten
to rave toben
raven rabenschwarz
raving mad total verrückt
to reason überlegen
to reassure versichern
to rebuke rügen, tadeln
to recall ins Gedächtnis rufen, sich erinnern
to receive erhalten, verliehen bekommen
receiver Telefonhörer
recently vor Kurzem
to reckon vermuten, glauben
to recognise (wieder)erkennen
reduction Preisnachlass
refund Rückerstattung
to refuse sich weigern
register Tonlage
to regret bereuen
reinforced verstärkt
relationship Beziehung
to relay wiedergeben, weiterleiten
release Befreiung
to release freilassen
relief Befreiung, Erleichterung
to remind erinnern (an)
rep Vertreter(in)
to repeat wiederholen
to replace zurücklegen
to report stolen als gestohlen melden
to reread (reread – reread) noch einmal lesen
to reroute weiterverbinden
to resent Ressentiments haben gegen
to resist widerstehen
resistance Widerstand
rest Pause, Ruhe
to rest aufstützen
to restrain festhalten, zurückhalten
to retire in Ruhestand gehen
retirement Pensionierung
to retreat sich zurückziehen
to retrieve wiedererlangen, herausbekommen
revelation Enthüllung
revenge Rache
revenue Einnahmen
revered verehrt

to revert to zurückkehren zu
to rewind (rewound – rewound) zurückspulen
to rig manipulieren
to ring (rang – rung) a bell jemandem bekannt vorkommen, etwas klingeln lassen
to rise (rose – risen) (to one's feet) aufstehen
robbery Raubüberfall
rueful reumütig
rugger Rugby
rumpled zerzaust
to run (ran – run) out of something etwas nicht mehr haben
runt Zwerg
ruthless schonungslos

S

to sacrifice opfern
saliva Speichel
scam Betrug
scared verängstigt
scarred verschrammt
scary furchterregend
scholarship Stipendium
scone brötchenartiges Mürbgebäck
to score (Punkte/Tore) erzielen
to scratch kratzen
to scribble kritzeln
scrum Gedränge
to scythe down niedermähen
search warrant Durchsuchungsbefehl
secret Geheimnis
security-conscious sicherheitsbewusst
sedative beruhigend
seductive verführerisch
to seek suchen
to seem scheinen
sensible vernünftig
separated abgetrennt
sermon Predigt
set-up Ablauf, Aufbau
to sever abbrechen
to shake (shook – shaken) one's head den Kopf schütteln
shape Körperform
to share with somebody mit jemandem teilen; jemandem mitteilen
sheaf Bündel
sheer steil
shelf Regal
to shiver erschauern, frösteln
shop floor Laden
shortcake Teegebäck
shrewd scharfsinnig
to shrug mit den Achseln/Schultern zucken
to shudder schaudern
shutter Verschluss; Fensterladen
sickly widerlich
to sift through something etwas durchgehen
sigh Seufzer
to sigh seufzen
to signal blinken
significant deutlich
to sign up for something sich für etwas anmelden/vormerken/engagieren lassen
single einziger, einzige
to sip nippen, in kleinen Schlucken trinken
skill Geschick, Können

slap Klaps
to slap schlagen
sledgehammer Vorschlaghammer
sleeve Ärmel
slender schmal
slicked-back geschniegelt
to slide (slid – slid) gleiten
slightly ein bisschen, leicht
slim schwach, dünn
to slip back zurückrutschen, zurückfallen
to slip off entwischen; herunterziehen
sliver Scheibchen
to slope down abfallen
slot Sendeplatz
to slump zusammensacken, -sinken
smart schick
smart-arse Klugscheißer
to snap knipsen
to snarl knurren
snatch Raub
sneer Spötter
to sniff around herumschnüffeln
soft spot Schwäche
to soil schmutzig machen
sole einzige(r)
someone with a grudge jemand, der eine alte Rechnung zu begleichen hat
sooner or later früher oder später
soothing besänftigend
space Platz
spacious geräumig
to spare erübrigen
speckled gesprenkelt
spectacles Brille
to speed up beschleunigen
to spell out buchstabieren
spice Gewürz
spiky-headed mit spitz abstehenden Haaren
to spill the beans plaudern, etwas ausplaudern
to spin (spun – spun) spinnen
spine Buchrücken
spiralling spiralförmig gewunden
to spoil stören, verderben
to spot entdecken
to spread (spread – spread) sich ausbreiten
to spread out ausbreiten
spree Amoklauf
spy-hole Türspion
square Viereck
squashed eingequetscht, eng
to squeeze (sich) quetschen
to squirm schaudern
stack Stapel
stairwell Treppenhaus
stake-out Observierung
stampede Massenpanik
stance Haltung
to start erschrecken, hochfahren
state Zustand
station Radiosender; Polizeirevier
stationary stehend
statuesque von klassischer Schönheit
staunch überzeugt
stay Aufenthalt
to stay put an Ort und Stelle bleiben
steel Stahl
steering-wheel Lenkrad
step Stufe
stiff fest

to stifle unterdrücken
stock Warenbestand
straight geradewegs
straightforward einfach, unkompliziert
to stroke streicheln
to struggle sich wehren
stuck festgeklemmt
stuff Zeug
to stuff (hinein)stopfen
stuffing Innenleben, Füllung
to stumble in hineinstolpern
stunned verblüfft
sturdy-looking stabil aussehend
to subside nachlassen
substantial beachtlich
to succeed in doing something es schaffen, etw. zu tun
sudden plötzlich
suffering Leid
to suffice genügen
sufficiently ausreichend
to suggest vorschlagen
suitable geeignet
sullen mürrisch
sultry heißblütig
to summon up hervorbringen, aufbieten
superior Vorgesetzte(r)
supervisor Kontrolleur(in)
to suppose annehmen
supposedly angeblich
surface Oberfläche, Fläche
surname Nachname
to suspect vermuten, den Verdacht hegen, verdächtigen
suspicious verdächtig
to swap tauschen
to swear (swore – sworn) schwören
swelling zunehmend
swift schnell
switch Schalter
switchboard Telefonzentrale
sympathetic verständnisvoll

T

tabloid Boulevardzeitung, -presse
to tag someone jemandem auf die Schliche kommen
to take (took – taken) it that davon ausgehen, dass
to take one's films to a same-day processor seine Filme am gleichen Tag entwickeln lassen
to take some beating schwer zu übertreffen sein
to take something back etwas zurücknehmen
to take up anfangen mit
tame lahm
to tap tippen, klopfen
tape Kassette, Band
to tap out a tattoo mit den Fingern trommeln
taste Geschmack, Geschmacksrichtung
taunt Schmähung
to tear (tore – torn) herausreißen
to tease quälen
temporary vorübergehend
to tempt in Versuchung führen
to tend to dazu neigen
tense angespannt
that's supposing vorausgesetzt
theft Diebstahl
thief Dieb(in)

thoroughly vollständig, gründlich
though jedoch
to threaten bedrohen
thrilled begeistert, außer sich vor Freude
thrilling spannend
throng Gedränge
thumb Daumen
to thump schlagen, ein dumpfes Geräusch machen
tight knapp, eng
to tilt kippen
timid schüchtern
tiniest winzigster, -e
to tip deuten
to tip back nach hinten kippen
to tip one's head mit dem Kopf deuten
to tip someone off jemandem einen Tipp geben
to toast someone jemandem zuprosten, auf jemanden trinken
top of the range Spitzenmodell
to torment quälen
to touch berühren
tourniquet Abschnürbinde
tousled zerzaust
towards in Richtung
trace Spur
track Titel
to track down ausfindig machen
trademark Markenzeichen
traffic lights Ampel
travel agent's Reisebüro
tray (Eingangs-)Korb
to trigger auslösen
to trot trotten
trough Tief, Tiefpunkt
to tug ziehen, zupfen
tuned to eingestellt auf
to turn out sich herausstellen
turntable Plattenteller
twinkle Blitzen, Funkeln
to twist drehen
twisted shut zusammengekniffen
twofold doppelt
two-piece Zweiteiler

U

ubiquitous allgegenwärtig, unvermeidlich
unavoidable unvermeidbar
under one's breath leise, im Flüsterton
undertaker Leichenbestatter
to undo (undid – undone) aufmachen, entriegeln
uniform gleichmäßig
unlawful ungesetzlich
unmarked nicht gekennzeichnet
unread ungelesen
unremarkable nicht bemerkenswert
unthreatening nicht bedrohlich
untidy unordentlich
to untie aufknoten
upon über
upright aufrecht
urgent dringend
to usher hineinführen
utterance Äußerung
utterly völlig

V

valid zulässig
value Wert
valve Verstärker, Röhre
vast überwältigend
veined with blood stark gerötet
victim Opfer
view Aussicht
vile widerwärtig
villain Schurke
visible erkennbar
volume Band; Lautstärke
to vote wählen
vowel Vokal

W

wad Bündel
wafting Hauch
to wail jammern
waist Taille
wanted (polizeilich) gesucht
war zone Kriegsgebiet
to wave winken, fuchteln
to wear (wore, worn) tragen
we could do with ... es wäre gut, wenn ...
well-paid gut bezahlt
well-preserved gut erhalten
to wheeze quietschen
to while away the time die Zeit vertreiben
to whip peitschen
to whisper flüstern
wholly gänzlich
wicked böse
wimp Schwächling, Weichei
winch Winde
to wind (wound – wound) back zurückspulen
windcheater Windjacke
windscreen Windschutzscheibe
to wink at someone jemandem zuzwinkern
wiring Kabel
wiry drahtig
wistful wehmütig
to withdraw (withdrew – withdrawn) entziehen; (Geld) abheben
without ohne
with respect mit allem Respekt
witness Zeuge
to worm one's way sich durchschlängeln
worth wert
would-be vermeintlich
to wrap (ein-/um-)wickeln
to wrinkle one's nose die Nase rümpfen
wryly ironisch

Y

yell Schrei
to yell schreien
yet doch
yon jener
youth Jugendlicher
Y-registered nagelneu